'*The Talent Factor* opens new horizons for those organiz~~~~
their managers who want to succeed t~
beyond. An extremely stimulating r
market both in the UK and the USA.
                                    Doug Rat~

'This book will be invaluable to anyone
company culture.'
                    Professor Rex Clark, Dean, Leeds Business School

'Terry Lunn has managed to bring fresh insights to some of the basic
issues facing businesses today . . . a valuable read for those senior
managers and directors wishing to succeed.'
                    Roger Burnell, Managing Director, Britannia Airways

'Terry Lunn has put talent back on the managerial agenda. His book
is a smooth meld of important ideas and telling insights fused in the
heat of considerable experience . . . his precise, relevant and timely
analysis will make sense to good senior managers and enlighten the
rest.'
                    David T H Weir, Director and Professor of Management,
                    University of Bradford Management Centre

'Terry Lunn is that rare animal in management studies – a successful
practitioner as well as a thinker. His book shows that 'Quality Pays'
for any business, only when it gives as much attention to its human
resources as to its capital. This is a vision of success which deserves
more than lip service.'
                    Michael Jackaman, Chairman, Allied-Lyons

'*The Talent Factor* is the cordon bleu recipe for everyone in every
company who realizes the benefit of being an Investor in People.'
                    Tom Farmer OBE, Chairman and Chief Executive,
                    Kwik-Fit Holdings plc

'In *The Talent Factor*, Terry Lunn has produced a practical book
about how to get the best out of people that will answer the
problems of many managers. But most of all he demonstrates the
direct link between good management of human resources and
improved profitability.'
                    Roger Eglin, Managing Editor, The Sunday Times

About the Author

Terry Lunn is a strong advocate that organizations wishing to survive in the 1990s will have to be increasingly talent-led and must focus on quality and service.

This is a viewpoint that he has consistently maintained in his extensive writing on management and personnel. He is probably best known as a frequent lead writer for *The Sunday Times* appointments section.

Terry Lunn commenced his working life at the age of 15 in the West Midlands coal field and in 1964 was awarded an Industrial Relations Scholarship to Ruskin College, Oxford.

Since then he has held a number of senior personnel posts within Cadbury Schweppes and Allied-Lyons and is currently Personnel Director of Joshua Tetley & Son Ltd.

He is a member of the Advisory Board of Sundridge Park Management Centre and was recently appointed as Honorary Visiting Fellow in Personnel Management to the University of Bradford Management Centre. He, therefore, brings together a rare balance of a background in trade unions and senior management, tempered with a touch of academic exposure.

Much sought after as a speaker, he spends a considerable amount of time speaking at events throughout the world.

R Calvert

THE TALENT FACTOR

Key Strategies for Recruiting, Rewarding and Retaining Top Performers

TERRY LUNN

KOGAN PAGE

To Marcus and Georgina

First published in 1992

Kogan Page Limited
120 Pentonville Road
London N1 9JN

© Terry Lunn 1992

British Library Cataloguing in Publication Data
A CIP record for this book is available from the British Library.

ISBN 0 7494 0802 2

Typeset by J&L Composition Ltd, Filey, North Yorkshire
Printed in England by Clays Ltd, St Ives plc.

Contents

PART 2   Using Reward as the Lubricant for Success

PART 3   What Managers Really Want and How We Can Give it to Them

Acknowledgements

Over some 37 years my career has taken me from the pit bottom to the boardroom. During that time I have had the good fortune to work with a number of outstanding managers, all of whom have had an influence on my approach to management and the thoughts and views I have expressed in this book. To all of them I owe a debt of gratitude.

In particular, I wish to acknowledge the influence of Dr Donald O Clifton and his team at SRI, the input of Louis Jenkins, Sandy Maxwell, Mike Scally of Lifeskills and Professor Rex Clark of the Leeds Business School. To Professor David Weir, Director of the University of Bradford Management Centre my special thanks for his encouragement and constructive criticism as this book evolved from first draft to its completion.

I am grateful to Kathleen Dobson for her help in typing the first draft and to Polly Ann Sladen for the many early mornings and evenings she spent typing all the subsequent amendments and re-drafts, her ready cooperation was valuable and greatly appreciated. To the team members of Joshua Tetley Personnel Department and, in particular, Lynne Sagar, Les Kitchen and Neville Atkinson, my thanks for their help in collating the research applicable to our work within Joshua Tetley.

To Doug Rath of Talent +, a special acknowledgement for all his valuable advice and assistance as well as his unfailing support and friendship over the last eight years.

Finally, to my wife Valda, my appreciation for her encouragement, support and great tolerance as I spent evenings and weekends over the last six months committing my thoughts to paper.

Terry Lunn
Burn Bridge, Harrogate
1992

Introduction

Throughout the Western world the relaxation of traditional trading frontiers, freer movement of capital, services and labour and greater competition from the Far East are forcing organizations to face up to the reality that survival is based not just on securing a competitive advantage but on establishing a *sustainable* competitive advantage.

To date, the principal reaction by organizations has been to seek to achieve that objective through actively engaging in quality and service initiatives.

While the issues of quality and service will continue to be of vital importance there is a growing acknowledgement that the quality of an organization's human resource philosophies and policies will be of equal importance in determining its ability to secure that sustainable competitive advantage. An acknowledgement not fuelled by altruism but by a bottom-line-driven realization that significant advances can be made in company growth and profitability by adopting a different approach to the management of people at work.

Aiding and abetting this process in the UK is the growing awareness that, whilst the Thatcher years resulted in a rebalancing of power between those managing and those managed, simply continuing policies of holding down wage costs and enforcing change through fear of recessionary unemployment is hardly a scenario for securing a greater contribution from employees through the 1990s.

In the USA increased competition from the Far East and Pacific Rim is making significant inroads into traditional home markets through innovation and higher product quality. Initial reaction to this has been an attempt to import into human resource strategies some of the key elements of those foreign cultures. The deficiencies of that philosophy are now becoming apparent and as a consequence, organizations are concluding that long-term solutions to the problems of managing people at work can only be achieved organically.

In continental Europe the collapse of the USSR has re-focused attention on individualism, a consequence of which is that systems based on collectivism and representational rights are under challenge. In particular, the co-determination policies of Germany, once heralded as a model for western economies, are coming under increasing scrutiny as management and employees alike question whether they enhance individual rights or simply subjugate them by enhancing the collectivist rights of the trade union movement.

More than ever before, implementing effective human resource strategies for the 1990s and beyond will require organizations to appreciate the fundamental need, and have the ability to:

- Recruit talent – this will inevitably entail organizations jettisoning conventional selection and recruitment systems as they come to terms with the fact that talent by its very nature is always going to be in short supply and a new approach to resourcing is required.

- Reward and recognize high performance – the requirement is for more imaginative and comprehensive systems for rewarding and recognizing high performance. The reality is, what happens in organizations is what we reward.

- Create the right expectations – organizations for the future need to understand more effectively and respond to individual expectations from work. The challenge is to enable the key motivators of responsibility, achievement and feelings of self worth, to become common currency throughout the organization rather than the preserve of the minority, accomplished in an environment where managers build productive relationships with all employees. In short, the ability of organizations to empower individuals at work will be an essential ingredient of success for the remainder of this century and beyond.

- Consciously invest in employees – this will involve organizations providing higher quality training and development and improved career management. The net result will be that in addition to increasing the organization's skill base it will be better equipped to retain its best performers.

THE TALENT FORMULA

The next requirement is for the four key components to be implemented as a comprehensive coherent strategy. As Michael Armstrong[1] points out, the history of personnel management, in fact management generally, over the last two decades is littered with techniques and nostrums such as management by objectives, job enrichment, quality circles, assessment centres and so on. Most of these failed to make any real impact on organizational performance, not because they were deficient in themselves, but because they were implemented piecemeal and used very often in isolation.

To reinforce the message that the four key components need to be implemented in a coherent and comprehensive manner the following formula can be constructed in applying our human resource strategy for the 1990s.

Talent × (Reward + Expectations + Investment) = People Productivity

In applying the formula we first need to recognize the primacy of talent in the equation and that the ability of the other components to act and interact to generate higher people productivity is governed by the level of talent. Secondly, we need to give the talent element a higher value than the other components. The overwhelming majority of managers, from their day to day experience, will have no difficulty in accepting that the talent factor should have a higher weighting in the equation. Evidence to support that viewpoint can be found in a recent study in the Journal of Applied Psychology[2] where a comparison was made between the productivity of the top 1 per cent performers compared with the average and the bottom 1 per cent. The findings of the study comparing the complexity of jobs were as follows:

Top 1 per cent productivity vs Average productivity

Low Complexity	The top performs 52% better than the average
Medium Complexity	The top performs 85% better than the average
High Complexity	The top performs 127% better than the average

Top 1 per cent productivity vs Bottom productivity

Low Complexity	The top performs 300% better than the bottom
Medium Complexity	The top performs 1,200% better than the bottom
High Complexity	Low performers cannot learn the job at all

Additional evidence to support the contention that the talent factor should enjoy a higher value can be found in the data from Joshua Tetley, Harman Management and the documented validity studies from the airline industry in Chapter 2.

Accordingly it is proposed that the value of the talent factor should be raised to the power of 2. The formula can therefore be described as follows:

$$T^2 \times (R + E + I) = \textbf{PEOPLE PRODUCTIVITY}$$

While the equation is not scientifically based it does parallel the validated work of Hunter, Schmidt and Judiesch. In any case, the prime purpose of the equation is to demonstrate the primacy of *talent* as a key determinant of organizational growth and profitability, and to enable us to better appreciate that in order to realize the full extent of individual potential we have to give equal time and attention to applying appropriate *reward*, creating the right *expectations* and *investing* in employees.

To appreciate the effect on people productivity of the factors contained in the talent formula, let us apply it on a 1–10 scale (with 10 high) to two representative, but far from hypothetical companies.

In company *A* the conventional face to face interview is used for determining hiring decisions. From studies both in the USA and the UK we know that approximately one third of those appointments will be of individuals of high talent, one third of the individuals will be of good to average ability and the remainder will be low performers. We can therefore apply a rating of 5 to the talent factor.

In terms of reward the company applies a highly centralized and structured payment system, leaving little scope for imaginative reward and recognition, therefore a value of 4 is ascribed to the reward element.

Since company *A* is a predominantly bottom line profit orientated organization enhancing satisfaction from work receives only limited endorsement from senior management and therefore we will award a value of 4 to the expectation element.

On training and development the entreaties and initiatives promoted by government departments and employers' associations have had an impact on the company's willingness to commit more resources to these areas. We will accordingly attribute a value of 8 to the investment element.

Applying those values to the equation the effect is:

$$T\,5^2 \times (R4 + E4 + I8)$$

giving a people productivity rating of 400.

In company *B* the prime focus in selection is to understand the key characteristics of the company's best performers and using objective selection systems they are able to identify which individuals possess the talents they are seeking. We will therefore apply a rating of 8 to the talent factor.

On reward, the emphasis is on rewarding the individual and as appropriate, team performance with imaginative pay, incentive and recognition schemes. We will accordingly ascribe a value of 7 to the reward element.

Motivation at work through giving employees opportunities for greater responsibility at work, ensuring that job design reflects individual needs for achievement and challenge, and opportunities for career development, both laterally and vertically have always enjoyed a high priority at company B. In view of this high level of commitment we will award a value of 9 to the expectation element.

Training and development whilst traditionally enjoying a high profile in the company has been subject to financial restrictions due to economic downturn in one of their prime foreign markets. However, overall investment in training has been satisfactory and we will attribute a value of 5 to the investment element.

Applying the talent formula to those values gives the following result:

$$T \ 8^2 \times (R7 + E9 + I5)$$

representing a people productivity rating of 1344 – a three-fold improvement over company A. As mentioned above, no precise mathematical claims are made for the formula, its principal purpose being to underline the fact that a comprehensive and coherent approach to human resource management is essential as well as endorsing the fact that from time to time we need to confront and confound conventional wisdom. On the latter point it is of significance that investing in talent has a disproportionate positive effect on increasing people productivity compared to training. The reality that a large number of organizations have still to come to terms with is the fact that their future growth and profitability will be more directly determined by their ability to select and retain talent, than the amount of resources committed to training. Equally organizations need to be more aware that improving the talent profile of the organization, regenerating reward systems and uplifting expectations can be achieved at a relatively lower cost than the heavy-weight injection of time and resources incurred by solely relying on training and development. This is not to argue that training and development are not important. Indeed, we shall later be stressing the need for increased funding in these areas, but the critical point that many organizations throughout the Western world have still to grasp is that while training refines and develops talent, it doesn't create it.

We shall be basing each of the following sections on the key components in the formula. To make them successful we need to create a climate in the organization that will enable them to be positively received.

CREATING THE CLIMATE

First, organizations need to practise, not just preach, long-term strategy. While most managers will be able to pull their three- or five-year company plan from the back of the bottom drawer of the filing cabinet, the reality is that very often their business decisions are based on last month's profit and loss account. This mentality is a consequence of the short termism of the stockmarket and financial institutions. The result is a frequent change in direction, the brake of financial control on investment being applied and then released so creating uncertainty and disillusionment at all levels in the company, hardly a scenario for high morale and commitment to the company's goals.

This may be considered a harsh judgement on organizations but evidence to support it can be found in a survey of 150 manufacturing companies conducted by the consulting group Ingersoll Engineers.[3] In the survey Ingersoll questioned managing directors, directors and general managers on their attitudes to change. The key factors they identified to make change successful were clear communication, commitment at all levels and vision and understanding, these 'soft issues' scoring more highly than the 'hard issues' of detailed initial planning and financial justification.

However, in contrast to these views, when questioned on the benefits they sought from these changes there was a far greater emphasis on short-term financial control than on medium- or long-term growth. As Brian Small, Managing Director of Ingersoll Engineers commented, 'it's difficult to escape the conclusion that most MD's are thinking and looking in one direction and in practice are walking in the opposite direction'.

In marked contrast to the '30 day mentality' adopted by a large number of European and American companies is the approach taken by leading Japanese organizations. There the approach to investment is very much one of taking a long-term perspective, innovating today for growth for the next generation.

Second, a company needs to appreciate the value of its human resources. The credibility of its people policies will be measured by the amount of resources it invests in its employees. We need to arrest the preoccupation of the accountancy and finance profession which sees people just as another overhead cost. The reality is that unlike plant and equipment which depreciates from the day of installation, people have the capacity to be among the few appreciating assets in the business.

Third, company boards, and the personnel and human resources function in particular, need to appreciate that there are no quick fixes in changing company culture. That they don't is demonstrated by the bandwagon, currently gaining momentum, of how to change your company culture through training. As Ken Perkowski of Mobil Corporation cogently argues:

> Culture is not transmitted through training. It can't be, training is for skill development. Senior Executives waving banners of cultural change won't cause change within the rank and file. It's only who gets hired, who gets promoted and what their daily behaviour demonstrates which can convince the rank and file that values are indeed changing and that a true culture shift is afoot.[4]

Fourth, we need to understand that one of the biggest obstacles to improving performance in the majority of companies is their preoccupation with failure. For so long the cultural strands that have intertwined top management across a broad spectrum of organizations have been rooted in the belief that the more we understand the causes of failure the more we will appreciate the ingredients that give rise to success. Our education systems equally bear a heavy responsibility for this situation with their emphasis on negativism and remedial training.

For most of us this process starts in the classroom where the emphasis is on the things we do wrong rather than the things we do right. Equally, while accepting that we have to possess a level of basic competence in a range of subjects, why is it that extra tuition is always reserved for those subjects we have little talent for, rather than for those we have a real ability in, and where extra tuition would make us excel even more. Again, why is it that at examination time the student who gains two grade As, three grade Bs and one grade F finds that teachers and parents alike focus wholly on the grade F result and totally ignore, or only give scant acknowledgement to, the five successes achieved?

The net result is that managers who, in their early careers, became students of what goes wrong in organizations, in later life become experts in failure. Since a number of them will subsequently rise to the top of their organizations, it's hardly surprising that organizational health checks reveal pronounced symptoms of lack of innovation, absence of risk taking, poor morale amongst subordinates and so on.

If the West is to regain its competitive edge in both domestic and world markets then we need to confront and confound this flawed philosophy and adopt in its place the sentiments underlying Bing Crosby's hit song of the 1940s:

> Accentuate the positive
> Eliminate the negative
> Latch on to the affirmative.

Of course, it goes without saying that from time to time we need to learn from our errors and mistakes but such activities come under the heading of remedial action.

Companies that wish to grow and prosper through to the year 2000 and beyond need to implant into their culture the success philosophy. This is a philosophy based on the principal belief that the only way to achieve success and replicate it again and again is by systematically studying successful situations and events. The identification of the key ingredients that led to increasing market share, successfully launching a new product, exceeding budgeted profit, completing a major recruitment drive, or introducing a comprehensive change by establishing new working practices, enables us to be better equipped to repeat it again and again. For more than a decade management gurus on both sides of the Atlantic have walked the business stage holding up a mirror to examples of international excellence. We need to turn the spotlight on our own organizations to discover and rediscover the things we do well.

As we scan the management horizon to catch the vision of success our gaze from time to time will be obscured by the images of outdated philosophies, the spectre of so called conventional wisdom or the views of false prophets. It is no contradiction of the doctrine of success to contest or confront such views; in fact, it's a necessary prerequisite if we are to put success back on the boardroom agenda.

The legacy of failing to provide the right climate and a coordinated human resource strategy is that in most companies the following problems and challenges can be identified.

MANAGEMENT – TODAY'S TEN BASIC CHALLENGES

1. The inability to recruit and select talent consistently.

2. Understanding what happens in organizations is what you reward.

3. How to reward positively and recognize the top performers.

4. Widespread dissatisfaction with the lack of promotional opportunities and the consequential plateauing of careers.

5. Lack of opportunity for individuals to develop their careers from specialist functions to generalists.

6. Managers wishing to exit from their current organizations to find a more challenging and fulfilling role.

7. Other forms of employment being viewed as more attractive than conventional careers.

8. Dissatisfaction with current management development systems and the level of training provided.

9. Insufficient regard as to the real cost of high management and staff turnover.

10. The inability to commit large sections of the workforce to the goal of becoming a quality and service driven organization.

REVIEWING THE ISSUES

In the following chapters we shall be seeking ways of addressing these issues through a better understanding and appreciation of the key components of talent, reward, expectation and investing in people. To achieve these aims this book has been divided into four sections.

In the first section we identify the uniqueness of talent and examine the inherent inadequacies of the most commonly used forms of selection. We will be proposing that if we are really desirous of recruiting talent into the organization then we need to study systematically our most successful performers through the process of structured interviews.[5] Furthermore, we need to give time and attention to fitting – casting that talent in areas of the business in which it will achieve its full potential.

In the second section we explore how to positively reward and recognize individuals so that we can optimize their contribution to the organization. In pursuit of the goal of making reward systems aspirational we shall call for conventional wisdom to be cast aside and jettison a number of prevailing attitudes to the subject of reward. These attitudes have been formed for a whole generation of executives and managers by the influences of centrally controlled pay policies, collectivism, appeasement by negotiation, the mistaken belief that social justice in organizations is achieved when we treat everyone equally and so on.[6]

To replace those attitudes and perceptions we shall be advocating that what happens in organizations is what we reward, and that soundly based reward and recognition programmes are the organizational lubricant for success. They must be soundly based in that they support the behaviour we are seeking to promote. The key triggers that generate reward must be capable of being directly influenced by the actions of those to whom the schemes apply. Finally we argue that to be effective, reward schemes have to be aspirational both in the amount they generate and the frequency of payment.

In the third section we review the two components of creating desirable expectations and investing in employees. It will be suggested that one of the key tasks of management is to harness the individual talent and potential that is available within the organization. It will be argued that to date we have been singularly unsuccessful in achieving that goal and that to a large extent the talent and potential that individuals bring to their workplace everyday lies untapped or underutilized.

Management dissatisfaction within organizations is widespread, but it is capable of being remedied. Among a range of solutions offered we shall focus on the need for companies to establish and convey a compelling vision of the organization's future, to provide sound and effective promotional and developmental opportunities whereby crossing functional boundaries becomes the norm, not the exception, and to inject more challenge and fulfillment into the roles individuals perform at work. In addition we shall turn our attention to the 'great training debate' and explode the myth that more means better, a point that still remains to be understood by Government and Opposition alike as they seek to politicize the whole subject of training and development. It will be argued that organizations need to understand that training and development enable management to build on strengths and develop talents but they cannot create them where they do not already exist.

In the fourth and final section we demonstrate that while the key to radically improving competitiveness, whether in domestic or international markets, is in providing excellent quality products and service, the reality in most companies is that the consumer is an afterthought. Despite the growth in customer service campaigns and initiatives during the 1980s it is estimated that up to 90 per cent of the programmes in existence have either failed or will fail in the near future. The symptoms of failure include the absence of clear objectives and measurement, insufficient commitment from the chief executive and his top management team, lack of resources to support the programme, inability to appreciate that service driven companies need to abandon the traditional control style of management in favour of an enabling style whereby management focus is on helping subordinates satisfy consumer's needs, and so on.

In order to overcome these problems six ingredients can be distilled which will enable companies to mount and maintain effective quality and service initiatives.

The link between quality and service and the previous sections is that customer service initiatives are no substitute for soundly based management and personnel policies and philosophies. In reality these are essential prerequisites to committing an organization to being the best provider of quality and service in its market sector.

REFERENCES

1 Armstrong, Michael (ed) (1992) *Strategies for Human Resource Management*, Kogan Page, London.
2 Hunter, Schmidt and Judiesch (1990) 'Individual differences in output variability as a function of job complexity', *Journal of Applied Psychology*, vol 75 (1).
3 Ingersoll Engineers Ltd. (1991) 'Change – the Good, the Bad and Visionary', a survey of organizational trends in the British manufacturing business, Rugby, Warwickshire.
4 Perkowski, K (1991) 'Heretics of TQM', Corporate Alliances, vol 1, no 1, 4th Quarter, published by Dalton Alliances Inc.
5 Lunn, T R (1987) 'A Scientific Approach to Selection', *Personnel Management*, October.
6 Lunn, T R (1989) 'How to Swing Unused Talent into Action', *Sunday Times*, 20 August.

► PART 1 ◄

Selecting Talent – Myth or Reality

1

Recruiting Talent or Just Filling Vacancies?

Talent is currently one of the most overworked words in the management vocabulary. So let us first of all define what we mean by it.

Talent is the capacity to achieve a near perfect performance. It results in desired spontaneous behaviour and is a natural ability, not primarily acquired through effort.

Its manifestations are many and varied and can be identified and discovered in a whole range of diverse individuals, jobs and professions. The typist who types a word perfect report, the waitress who greets customers with a warm friendly smile and provides excellent service again and again, or the project manager who brings a large complex project to completion on time, on budget with quality the constant, are all examples of talent in action. As is the chief executive who out of a whole range of strategic options selects the one that maximizes long-term profit and growth, or the lathe operator who can manufacture to specification first time, or the medical consultant who, due to a blend of surgical skills and talent for building relationships with patients, enjoys a higher and faster patient recovery rate than his less talented colleagues.

Defined in this way it is relatively easy to remove a number of popular misconceptions; namely that talent is somehow dependant on academic qualifications, class or social background. The reality is that talent comes in every human size and shape and from backgrounds that have been both educationally advantaged and deprived.

The ability of organizations consistently to identify and select talent is the key discriminator between success and mediocrity, yet the majority of management pay only lip service to this notion. This is despite the fact that there is a clear correlation between company performance and the ability to recruit and retain talent.

It is no accident that organizations such as Mercedes, 3M, Marks and Spencer, Mars, Disney and the Marriott Hotel Group have been able to maintain their position as the consumer's number one choice in their respective market sectors – rather, it's a reflection of their single-minded determination only to recruit talent and to invest sufficient resources in their people. What they have discovered and what other organizations have still to understand is the simple truth that employing talent makes a difference to the bottom line. There is no exclusivity, no secret about the point, it was after all 65 years ago that Bingham and Freyd told us that

> the successful employee . . . does more work, does it better, with less supervision, with less interruption through absence . . . He makes fewer mistakes, and has fewer accidents . . . He accordingly learns more quickly, is promoted more rapidly and stays with the company.[1]

As Lee Iacocca, of the Chrysler Organization has succinctly put it: 'Hire the best, nothing will make a chief executive look smarter than having a talented management team around him'.

Out of all the key decision making activities that chief executives and their senior board members are involved in, the ability to recruit talent and weld it into a winning team is paramount.

Among a whole host of evidence available to support that view is the recent study commissioned by Korn-Ferry International and Columbia University Graduate School of Business.[2] Believed to be one of the most comprehensive studies of executive leadership, one of its principal findings is that 'the human resources function must play a more central role in the strategic recruitment and development of exceptional executives'.

It further stresses that effective human resource management is becoming so critical to corporate success and survival that companies must view executive recruitment as seriously as the prospect of corporate merger or acquisition.

THE CONVENTIONAL INTERVIEW

Are companies equipped to identify the talent they so desperately require? A report by the Institute of Manpower Studies (IMS)[3] on employee selection in the UK contains grounds for disquiet.

As anticipated, it found that the conventional face to face interview was the most widely used method of selection with over 90 per cent of the survey's respondents using it for selecting managerial and professional staff.

Of particular significance is the IMS finding that over 96 per cent of the respondents felt it was either 'very reliable' or 'quite reliable'. This is despite the fact that research consistently shows the opposite to be true. As the report itemizes, there is well-founded and 'widespread doubt about interviewer validity and reliability'.

That there is widespread doubt on the efficiency of the face to face interview to predict future job success is hardly surprising given the following facts:

- Many interviewers spend insufficient time preparing for and understanding the success criteria for the job to be filled. If they don't understand the attributes that lead to success, how can they determine which candidate possesses them?

- Interviewers frequently spend over 60 per cent of the time talking, and a further 20 per cent of the time thinking about the next question to be asked and then have the affrontary to say how much they have learned about each candidate. The whole point of the interview is to listen to the candidate – nothing is learned by talking.

- The judgement of interviewers is often affected by candidates with a high level of interpersonal skills but little else, or by the halo effect of physical appearance. So often, if judgement is affected by personal appearance, all that is achieved is simply to hire a new business suit or designer dress into the organization.

- A whole list of questions is often prepared but interviewers are unsure of how to evaluate the responses they elicit. A common feature of panel interviews is that interviewers often have three of four 'pet' questions to which they subject each candidate. Even though these questions elicit a range of contradictory responses, they seem oblivious to that fact when compiling their preferred short list.

- Interviewers typically make up their mind about a candidate within the first four minutes of an interview with prejudice rarely being swayed by subsequent factual information.

- A candidate's non-verbal behaviour in the interview can very often be more important in determining its outcome than experience or qualification.

The conclusion is that, used in isolation, the conventional face to face interview is unlikely to be of much use in identifying the talent companies so desperately need.

PERSONALITY TESTS

In an attempt to inject more objectivity into the selection system, a growing number of companies are turning to other systems. But are they, often at great cost, merely exchanging one problem for another?

The fastest growing selection technique over the last ten years has been the personality test. IMS estimates that some 50 per cent of companies in the UK are using personality testing as part of their selection process. The most commonly used include: Kostick Perception and Preference Inventory (PAPI), Personal Profile Analysis System (PPAS) and Occupational Personality Questionnaire (OPQ). However, despite the claims of their originators or their selling agents, personality tests are not without their critics and a number of reservations have been expressed on the reliability of such tests and the validity of their construction.

Many tests have been constructed on cross-sections of the population, or specific groups within the population – university students, members of the armed forces etc – which while assisting researchers in capturing their data quickly have precious little relevance when you are using such tests to select departmental managers, salesmen, and so on. Alternatively they are based on consultants' perceptions or, even worse, averages.

And what is an average? 'It's the best of the worst and the worst of the best'. Yet, when we started the whole recruitment process, didn't we commit ourselves to selecting only the best?

Concern has also been expressed as to whether such tests elicit answers which describe a candidate's personality accurately or merely result in individuals giving what they consider to be 'socially desirable' answers. For example, a candidate for a salesman's job might reasonably assume that an extrovert character would be a beneficial response and, accordingly, skew his response to questions which ask for self assessment against such traits.

But it is the area of how valid such tests are as predictors of job performance that has raised the most concern. The pre-eminent figures in raising the awareness of personnel practitioners to the potential problems in this area have been Steve Blinkhorn and Charles Johnson. From a study of the three most widely used personality tests in the UK they conclude that 'whilst they may be invaluable for counselling purposes or in other situations where self perception is as important as the truth, we see precious little evidence that even the best personality tests predict job performance'.[4]

ASSESSMENT CENTRES

The third area has been the growing use of the assessment centre, which has its roots in officer selection in pre-war Germany. Widely used by the Regular Commission and Civil Service Boards, it is attracting a growing number of adherents in industry. Assessment centres have been defined as a 'process by which an individual, or group of individuals, is assessed by a team of judges using a comprehensive and integrated series of techniques'.[5]

Conventionally, assessment centres use both group and individual exercises. As Mark Cook[6] describes, individual exercises divide into three areas. The 'in tray' assesses the quality of decisions, the ability to plan, to organize and delegate. The 'irate customer/employee' exercise evaluates the ability to analyze and interpret facts and effectively demonstrate interpersonal skills. The third area is the 'sales presentation' where the candidate attempts to sell to a sceptical, challenging customer.

Group exercises are divided into three components. The 'assigned role exercise', in which each candidate has an individual brief to compete for an unequal share of the groups resources or to get the group to accept their policy on a specific issue, is used to assess negotiating skills, persuasiveness and ability to compromise. 'Unassigned role exercises', such as running a simulated business in which market conditions, production capacity and so on are frequently changed seek to assess individuals' ability to cope with stress and uncertainty and to show a clear sense of direction and focus. In 'team exercises' the group divides into two, one group advocating one particular viewpoint, and the other half the opposing case. Such exercises are very often based on collective bargaining case studies with one group role playing management and the other the role of trade union representatives, the exercise being used to evaluate negotiating skills, ability to solve problems and work as a team.

Although assessment centres tend to be rated favourably by candidates and participating companies alike, they do have a number of drawbacks. Professor Peter Herriot of Sundridge Park Management Centre defines two major problems in their use.

First, 'assessors often fall into the trap of believing they are measuring the qualities displayed by candidates when, in fact, they are simply rating how well they perform the task they were given'. Second, 'research shows that, even if assessors have up to 12 qualities they require candidates to possess, they will often only take into account two of three of them in their final judgement'.

A further problem is that properly researched and validated assessment centres are not inexpensive to install and, as a consequence, a number of cheap off-the-shelf systems are being sold and installed by less than scrupulous consultancies. Such systems are to be avoided since all the research evidence shows that assessment centres need to be designed for the organization/job in question.

It therefore follows that the use of generic criteria and/or off-the-shelf data cannot either be properly described as an assessment centre[7] or claim necessarily to have the predictive validity or acceptability of one.

STRUCTURED INTERVIEWS

One selection system that is attracting a growing number of adherents and few critics is structured interviews. From the systematic study of successful performers in a wide variety of jobs, ranging from senior executives to sales staff, parish priests to pub managers, airline cabin crew to accountants, dentists to drivers, the system enables the identification of the key characteristics that make these individuals successful.

This is where the process clearly distinguishes itself from other selection systems in that the data used in structured interviews is based on an organization's most successful operators – the talent we want more of. The system also provides separate structured interviews for each occupational group which enables interviewers to identify to what degree individual applicants possess these characteristics.

Life themes

The identification of an individual's characteristics – the talents they possess – is based on their 'life themes'. A life theme is a consistent, recurring pattern of thought, feeling and behaviour.

Dominant themes characterize people. While up to now most managers will have been unfamiliar with the concept of life themes, in reality they are already part of our everyday vocabulary. We continually characterize our colleagues, our subordinates or our superiors, by reference to their dominant themes. We also use themes as a shorthand to describe figures of history: Kennedy – vision; Churchill – courage; Mother Theresa – compassion. From the world of entertainment we will talk of the artistry and dedication of Dame Kiri Te Kanawa, the creativity of Andrew Lloyd Webber or the exactness and agility of Torville and Dean.

In our everyday business life we adopt the same process when we describe those we come into contact with. When we characterize our favourite waitress as having a burning desire to win approval from customers, our top salesman as having the ability to build long-term relationships with clients, our top delivery crew as having high stamina, or our chief executive as being a visionary, then we are on to themes.

Donald O Clifton, President of SRI, maintains that theme activity can be generated internally, demonstrated by the individual going in pursuit of the behaviour appropriate to the theme. On the other hand the theme can be spontaneously aroused by stimuli which afford it satisfaction.

Who wants to win customers?

So, some individuals have a proclivity for winning customers – or what we would call a 'customer woo' theme. Take, for example, a pub or restaurant manager who goes in search of customers in order to talk to them or win their approval or, when faced with a customer at the counter, such individuals will stop whatever they are doing in order to serve them. Irrespective of other priorities, the need to serve is paramount. In short, the theme is dominant and is not satisfied until the individual has served the customer.

Contrast that with the situation where the salesperson has low woo. When we approach they display symptoms of customer indifference; they will turn away from us, avoiding eye contact; check the stock; or talk to another sales assistant. Do we go back? We do not!

Consider the hotel chains which spend large sums on glitzing up their hotel reception areas and then staff them with the non-smilers of life. When we stand at the reception desk, waiting to be registered or to be checked out, the indifference we face from such staff as they attend to their priorities of personal telephone calls, breaking off the transaction to attend to interruptions from other members of staff, our eyes focus again on the reception area. As we stand in line, getting more and more frustrated, the reception area, which once radiated style and ambience, becomes more and more tarnished. The impact that the hotel management was trying to achieve and invested substantially in has been eradicated by the selection of staff who are the natural lighthouse keepers of life rather than the natural greeters of customers.

A shining beacon in the sea of indifference we all too often experience in hotels is Theo Athanasiou the Concierge at The Annabelle, a hotel in Paphos, Cyprus. The genuine smile that radiates his face as he welcomes guests both old and new could illuminate a room. He sets an example for all the staff that customers count and the pay off is that The Annabelle enjoys a repeat booking rate during the shoulder months of May and October of up to 40 per cent. Operating in the notoriously fickle upmarket package holiday sector it's a record its competitors would love to emulate.

Spotting natural talents

Although companies have become more appreciative of the correlation between high morale of employees and company profitability, insufficient regard has been paid to selecting executives and managers who have a natural talent for building productive relationships with staff.

Individuals who have a 'relator' theme will consciously seek out opportunities to invest time in their staff. They see them as team players and invariably enjoy high morale. In contrast, the low relator manager will keep staff at arm's length, avoid social contact, see them as people who perform tasks. Such an individual will almost certainly experience low morale and high labour turnover.

As the importance of training and management development has moved up the management agenda, companies are spending large sums on training their managers to be better developers of subordinates. How effective this will be remains open to question. Surely, if being a developer of subordinates is to be a key attribute of our management cadre, our selection systems should enable us to select those with a natural talent for developing others – those that possess the 'developer' theme.

Individuals with that talent are always looking for opportunities whereby staff can experience personal growth and take genuine satisfaction in seeing subordinates promoted. In contrast, managers who have a low developer theme tend to restrict an individuals growth; they experience fear symptoms when faced with individuals who have superior talents. Organizational growth for them is never seen as being the sum total of the growth of individuals in the organization.

Relevant themes

Sets of themes are appropriate to each profession, vocation or set of tasks to be achieved. For example, a salesman has a set of themes, an area manager a different set and a finance director a further set of themes. For use in the selection process the relevant themes for each group are established by careful research and, in particular, by conducting 'focus groups' with the most successful performers in the organization and their senior managers and directors.

Commenting on the advantages of studying people's themes, Susanne Lawrence, editor of *Personnel Management*, says that 'the act of studying people's talents and focusing on them can actually stimulate and develop their talents; they can be motivated by talking about them. Concentrating on themes also assists people to manage their weaknesses; and teams can be built by putting together people with complementary strengths'.

In order to establish to what degree an individual candidate possesses the relevant themes, a structured interview is conducted, based on a set of pre-determined questions which must be asked in the same way for each person interviewed. For every question there is a particular element to listen for in the answer, this being the essence of what successful people in that particular profession or vocation say when they respond to the same question. This is the key feature of the system because it is all about selecting people with success potential.

The system is designed so that people within a company or organization can be trained to administer and analyze the results of the interview. This significantly increases the degree of understanding and commitment of users, compared with other systems which require analysis by external organizations.

Potential problems and challenges

In implementing structured interviews we need to be aware of the following potential problems and challenges. First, since the interview is modelled on outstanding talent, exemplars have to be carefully identified. Unlike a number of other systems structured interviews cannot be developed from the general population. Second, validation is critical, as in all forms of effective psychometric measurement, and it can take time to identify appropriate performance criteria.

Third, good interviewers have to be identified and carefully trained. They can be hard to find, since their talent profile will contain ethics, pride, discipline, woo, empathy, work orientation, team work; a combination of qualities that is not common. However, as is demonstrated later in this section the impact on company performance if structured interviews are implemented successfully is considerable.

SUMMARY

In this chapter we have concluded that:

- Talent needs to be defined more precisely and we have accordingly defined it in such a way that we can readily appreciate that talent has no respect for social class, age or educational background.

- The ability of organizations to identify and select talent is the key determinant governing long-term growth and profitability. However, in our review of the three most widely used selection systems, serious deficiencies were recognized, deficiencies that place a real question mark over their effectiveness in consistently selecting talent.

- Most of those shortcomings can be avoided by using structured interviews, since the system is based on a systematic study of the most successful performers in the particular job or profession.

- The concept of life themes, which is the core element of the structured interview process, provides the means by which we are better able to identify and distinguish the many forms of talent we witness every day of our lives.

REFERENCES

1 Bingham, W V and Freyd, M (1926) *Procedures in Employment Psychology*, Shaw, Chicago.
2 'The 21st Century Report' (1989) Korn/Ferry (See also Trigg, P R 1991 'Human Resources Function and Business Schools', *Update* vol 7, June, Drake Bean Morin Ltd).
3 Beven, S and Fryatt, J (1988) 'Employment Selection in the UK', Report No. 160, December, Institute of Manpower Studies.
4 Blinkhorn, S and Johnson, C (1990) 'The Insignificance of Personality Testing', *Nature*, December.
5 Fletcher, G (1982) 'Assessment Centres' in Mackenzie-Davey, D and Harris, M *Judging People*, McGraw-Hill, UK.
6 Cook, M (1989) *Personnel Selection and Productivity* John Wiley, New York.
7 Dale, M and Iles, P (1992) *Assessing Management Skills*, Kogan Page, London.

2

Stop Poaching, Start Rescuing

My own company's interest in improving our selection methods was stimulated by the decision in 1983 by Allied Breweries, the brewing division of Allied-Lyons, to transform the business from a product-orientated company to a customer service company. Each trading company (of which Joshua Tetley is one) was charged with implementing that strategic decision. We had clear evidence that there was a direct correlation between the employment of talented people in our 1100 pubs and the results achieved, but there was no objective system for analyzing or selecting candidates who possessed those talents.

In order to investigate fully all the possible ways of improving our selection system, we set up a working party made up of retail line management and personnel and training specialists. The decision to involve both line and staff functions was deliberate in that this is essential in any radical change process if it is to be subsequently successfully implemented.

Perhaps one of the important lessons that the personnel function has still to learn is that, while it can be the innovator and the catalyst for change, successful implementation lies wholly in the hands of line colleagues.

As part of the working party's activities, a study tour of the USA was arranged since that country is generally acknowledged to be at the leading edge of customer service. As part of the tour, field visits were arranged to ten companies that enjoy a particularly high reputation for customer service and hospitality, including Baskin-Robbins, Walt Disney Corporation and Wendy's.

It was during a visit to Chicago, hosted by the American Restaurant Association, that the party came into contact with a leading group of consultant psychologists who gave a presentation on their company's work on the selection of talent for the hospitality industry. The opportunity for discussing a system that would enable us to understand more clearly why a number of our pub managers were more successful than others and allow us to select recruits who displayed the same talents as our most successful operators was of immediate interest. That interest was stimulated by our meeting Ed Eynon, Vice President, Human Resources for American Woodmart, who was able to demonstrate, from his experience of using structured interviews for almost a decade, a direct correlation between the selection of talent and the impact on company profitability.

Further confirmation of the effectiveness of structured interviews was provided by Golden Corrall, an American restaurant group which had been using the system for eight years for the selection of restaurant managers and staff. The detailed information they supplied was evidence for us that the system had been a major factor in improving restaurant takings and profit and had reduced staff turnover.[1]

Based on this initial contact and further in-depth discussion, a proposal was worked out for testing the system in the UK. In fact, it was to be the first time it had been used in the UK and the exploratory research was initiated at Joshua Tetley in September 1983.

It is worth noting here that our interest considerably predated and was thus totally unrelated to the subsequent, and, in some organizations, the short-term, fashionable preoccupation with 'excellence' and customer service.

The research involved the establishment of four 'focus groups' in which pub managers, area managers, trade directors and personnel and training staff discussed their experience in the trade, focusing on successful situations and highly productive people. In addition, 50 of our most successful pub managers were asked to attend in-depth interviews. Their selection was based on objective data including profit and sales turnover as well as the individual rating given by area managers on day to day performance.

THEMES OF SUCCESSFUL MANAGERS

From that study, 18 themes were identified which we hypothesized were predictive of a pub manager's ability to be successful.

1. *Mission* – having purpose and meaning in work that goes beyond the tangible rewards to attaining a satisfaction from the service provided.
2. *Focus* – goal persistence, or a thoughtful and effortful continuation of activity towards the goal.
3. *Performance orientation* – the performance orientated pub manager not only likes to know the direction he or she is going in but also likes figures or scores to measure progress.

4. *Pride* – derives from a person's ego drive which is best defined as a person's need to define himself or herself as a significant person and provides a clear insight into an individual's level of competitiveness.
5. *Growth orientation* – the high growth orientated person has a tendency to extend and increase whatever it is that he or she is focused on doing. Put him or her in the least likely situation where the status quo has existed for years and, within minutes, the growth oriented managers says 'How do you get this thing going?'.
6. *Critical thinking* – attempts to get at what is usually described as 'common sense'.
7. *Responsibility* – to take ownership for your own talents and your impact on other people and other things.
8. *Assertiveness* – the pub manager high in assertiveness can be direct and can take charge of others, usually without offending them.
9. *Mastery* – the pub manager high in mastery can define himself or herself through competency in performance.
10. *Versatility* – can accommodate a wide variety of situations. He or she is willing to do all kinds of work that must at one time or another be done in a pub.
11. *Stamina* – can endure the long hours that are required in a pub. Physical activity is satisfying to the high stamina person.
12. *Relator* – the good relator pub manager invests in their spouse, bar staff and customers in that order by being empathetic, listening and demonstrating awareness.
13. *Developer* – the good developer takes satisfaction from perceiving growth in staff.
14. *Customer woo* – essential in making the customer feel welcome when they enter a pub. The person high in customer woo wants everyone to like him or her because this helps the customer have a good time and want to come back to the pub.
15. *Stimulator* – the high stimulator pub manager tends the emotional environment by being enthusiastic, using humour, knowing the contagion of laughter and fun of competitive games.
16. *Arranger* – the good arranger is continuously coordinating the resources of the pub to a particular purpose. Activities are planned, teams are built and activities are implemented.
17. *Ethics* – has to do with honesty, integrity and keeping promises. Pub managers who are high in ethics do what they say they will do.

18. *Compatibility* – has to do with the capacity of a licensee and partner to find fulfilment individually while working together in managing.

ASK THE RIGHT QUESTIONS

The pub manager selection system was constructed on the basis of six questions related to each theme, together with the elements to listen for in the responses to each question. These, as will be remembered, equate to what successful people in that particular profession say when they respond to that question. Obviously, to disclose these would be to invalidate the process but, just as an example, when assessing the degree of focus an applicant has, we would ask 'What do you want to accomplish in the next five years?'. What we would look for in answer would be clear goals relating to success in our business, defined usually by managing a larger unit or bigger, more successful pubs.

In assessing how responsible an individual is we would ask 'At what age did you have the opportunity to take real responsibility?'. Our research indicates that our most successful operators sought and took responsibility at an early age and, in addition, were able to quite clearly identify what that responsibility was.

In terms of tapping into an individual's stamina, we would ask them about their hobbies and special interests, we would listen, say, for reference to activities that point to stamina and physical fitness. This might not be critical in all occupations, but pub managers work long hours and can't afford to get tired and fractious as the evening wears on. The study showed a clear correlation between success on the job and participation in physical activities during leisure time.

In validating the predictability of the system, a further 100 pub managers and their partners were rated on a scale of A to D, based on pub performance – takings, profit and staff turnover. Without being privy to these ratings, the team then rated the individuals on the same scale of A to D using the pub managers selection system. Only then was the classification arising from the pub performance ratings correlated with classifications arising from the results of the selection system. The standard for confidence in the strength of the coefficient of correlation was set out and agreed at 0.27. The coefficient that actually resulted was 0.54. This, as far as we were concerned, affirmed the value of the selection system for predicting success and, in 1984, structured interviews were launched within Joshua Tetley.

CHANGE YOUR ADVERTISING

The implications of committing an organization to recruiting only talent are far reaching. First we have to accept that we are seeking to recruit from the top 20 per cent in a particular occupational grouping. This has an immediate impact on the traditional resourcing methods used and requires us to look at fresh alternatives.

During the experimental stage of introducing structured interviews at Joshua Tetley, traditional advertising copy (Figure 2.1) was used in a variety of local and regional press, focusing on and tapping into the phrase 'management opportunities'. This type of advert generated a poor response in terms of the number of applicants, with no candidates recommended for appointment.

Figure 2.1 Traditional advertising copy

It's also salutary to note that the request to 'give brief details of why you think you're the best couple for the job' received little response from candidates in terms of either quality or quantity. On reflection, this was hardly surprising; successful people in any job or profession are normal, active, committed individuals and to be asked to do more than forward their CV will result in their turning over to the next page of job adverts.

For those companies who continue to include in their advertising copy such phrases as 'please outline in detail how you meet our requirements', it certainly raises the question of how worthwhile this approach is and, perhaps more importantly, how many good candidates they screen out by so doing.

As an alternative, the company launched a series of 'come and meet us' campaigns using themed adverts. This approach used recruitment advertising to invite potential candidates to meet company representatives and undertake a preliminary screening interview. Critical to the success of the exercise has been the style and wording of the advertisement (Figure 2.2) promoting the campaign.

In the advert below the first four statements relate to four of the themes that we know appeal to successful potential candidates:

Figure 2.2 'Come and meet us' advertising

Statement	Theme
'Would you like the opportunity to run a successful business with a turnover in excess of £150,000?'	growth orinetation
'Do you take pride in every job you do and have to do better than previous records to feel that you are successful?'	pride/ego
'Do other people see you as dependable, as one who will grasp quickly what needs to be done?'	responsibility
'Can you create an atmosphere where people can have a good time night after night?'	stimulator/woo

Stimulating talent

Individuals who have a talent in these areas have their interest stimulated when they see statements such as those described. This is perhaps the key to themed adverts in that it not only screens out those who cannot relate to such statements but also, and more importantly, screens in those who have the talents being sought.

Using this type of advert has enabled Joshua Tetley to attract a whole range of candidates from the blue and white collar sections as well as from the professions, a number of whom have said that they had never before seriously considered being in the licensed trade – it was the advert that stimulated their interest.

In contrast, most traditional adverts merely seek to screen out less preferred candidates through the use of artificial age limits and educational and experience requirements, most of which are not representative of the best in-company performers. Little or no attempt is made to list the attributes that successful candidates are required to possess, thereby positively screening in talent.

It's perhaps hardly surprising that most of the recruitment advertising awards in the UK focus on the quality of the artwork and the razzamatazz of the copy, with little or no reference being made to how successful the advertisement was in attracting high calibre recruits.

It should, however, be stressed that producing themed adverts is no quick fix. It regularly takes up to three hours to design and produce the key questions and satisfy ourselves that we are hitting the key themes we require of candidates. Nevertheless, that time

TELESALES & CUSTOMER SERVICE MANAGER

circa £17,000

* *Do you enjoy motivating a team to achieve their goals and maximise their potential?*

* *Are you a highly organised and disciplined person?*

* *Do you strive to achieve more than is necessarily expected of you?*

* *Can you gain the commitment of others whilst maintaining a close relationship with them?*

If you can answer Yes to these questions, then you should be talking to us.

Joshua Tetley & Son Ltd is a highly successful trading company within Allied Breweries Ltd, operating throughout Yorkshire and the North East. The Company is a market leader with such quality products as Tetley Bitter, Castlemaine XXXX, Skol and Lowenbrau amongst its range.

The Telesales & Customers Service Manager will be responsible for improving the operating effectiveness of the Department, achieving sales performance targets and ensuring high standards of customer service through a team of approximately 20 people.

You should have a proven track record of success in a sales/customer orientated environment; experience of managing a team; be educated to 'A' level standard; and be aged 25-40. Familiarity with computer-based systems is desirable.

In return, we offer an excellent package, including BUPA, drinks allowance, non-contributory pension and relocation expenses, where appropriate.

Written applications, giving all relevant details including current salary, should be sent to:-

Miss K.W. Maxfield, Personnel & Training Officer, Joshua Tetley & Son Ltd., P.O. Box 142, The Brewery, Leeds LS1 1QG.

EST 1822

JOSHUA TETLEY & SON LIMITED

Figure 2.3 Examples of themed adverts

commitment is a worthwhile investment in terms of the results we achieve. Themed adverts of the type instanced in Figure 2.2 regularly produce up to 200 candidates, with a success ratio of one recommended for employment for every five applicants.

This type of advertising also works across a whole range of job vacancies, as illustrated in Figure 2.3 (opposite and above).

REFERRING TALENT

A further innovation in resourcing methods at Joshua Tetley was the use of referrals. This involves our area managers referring to the personnel department any candidates they have observed in a work situation who they believe have the talent to become successful pub managers.

This method can be highly effective once you have got over the initial reluctance to indulge in what many managers see as 'poaching' – think of it as 'rescuing' individuals and suddenly we all feel more comfortable about it.

The second objection is that individuals won't respond. The clear evidence is that they will and do. Why should individuals who are working in stores, petrol stations, restaurants be any different from their senior managers who are flattered by the approach from the head-hunter?

Equally, we now understand that it takes talent to spot talent and the higher the talent rating managers possess themselves, the more likely they are to identify that ingredient in others. Using talented managers as a source of referral is also a powerful means of influencing individuals to join your company. Talent is attracted to talent and everyone wants to join a winning team.

The data shows that referrals are a very effective method of resourcing with a success ratio of one recommended candidate for every three applicants.

NEVER STOP RECRUITING

One of the crucial implications for companies that wish to commit themselves to recruiting only talent is that you never stop recruiting. In a world of economic downturn, with consequential restrictions on recruitment, this might seem an odd proposition. It's certainly at odds with the practice of most human resources departments that only recruit when they have an identified vacancy. The reality is that once the scarce resource of talent is discovered by a company it should establish a relationship with the individual concerned so that, when a vacancy arises, they can speedily respond with a high calibre candidate. Companies that appreciate that fact will record the details of such individuals in a talent bank and maintain contact through sending them copies of important news bulletins and the company newsletter.

To some companies the correlation between recruiting talent and company performance is seen as so important that they will go over-establishment to attract the right individual.

One such company is the Thanos Group which operates a number of hotels in Cyprus. Their Managing Director Alecos Michaelides says: 'When I see an individual with outstanding talent, I imme-diately seek to hire him or her irrespective of our recruitment situation. Once you get that talent on board, the right vacancy will come up'.

The grapevine

'Off-the-street' unsolicited applications, enquiring about possible employment, are a continuing feature of the 1990s, the success ratio of this type of applicant being originally 13 candidates to one recommended for employment. However, increasing public awareness – the grapevine – that we are operating a unique form of selection has screened low talent out and high talent in and has improved our success ratio in recruiting pub managers by this method to seven to one.

Whilst the success ratio for the different resourcing methods referred to will be judged as highly effective by UK standards, how do they compare with international standards? Based on the experience of American companies recruiting for similar positions in the hospitality industry, a success ratio of 13 to one is judged to be satisfactory. Therefore, by these standards the UK experience can been seen as highly effective, particularly when we take into account the fact that in the main we are recruiting couples.

The further implication of these results is that it gives a lie to the commonly held belief that, by an act of evangelical intervention, all the individuals who are able to give excellent customer service reside in North America. The reality, irrespective of where in the world you are recruiting, is that *time is the variable – talent is the constant.*

TALENT EQUALS PROFIT

A further crucial question is whether 'talented' people make a better contribution to company profitability than individuals selected through the conventional face to face interview. In evaluating the performance of licensees selected through structured interviews, the key indicators we have used are total sales, controllable expenses, controllable profit and house net profit. We have compared the performance of this group with the performance of the previous licensee in each case and the average performance of the remainder of the managers selected through a conventional interview. The results of the 1986/87 financial year compared with the previous year are shown in Table 2.1.

Table 2.1 Performance of Pub Managers Selected through Structured Interview compared with Conventional Recruitment

	Structured interview	*Conventional recruitment*
Total sales	+12%	+2%
Controllable expenses	+14%	+5%
Controllable profit	+25%	+5%
House net profit	+17%	+8%

While the data is significant in itself, there is clear evidence that our best managers continue to develop and expand their business, considerably out-performing those managers with low talent. During the last five years we have compared the performance of our top 25 talented managers with our bottom 25 managers.

The results of the survey show that our top talented managers over the five years increased their profit by 166 per cent, our low talented managers by 55 per cent.

One common feature of the current recession is companies seeking to reduce their cost base by reducing the number of people employed, very often the reduction being achieved by voluntary redundancy exercises. While such voluntary programmes reduce the employee relations consequences of large-scale redundancy, is indiscriminate labour shedding in an organization's long-term interest?

Evidence to suggest that it may not be is demonstrated by a British retail company operating in the north-west that recently compared the relationship between the level of individual talent and profit performance over the period 1989–90 to 1990–91.

The analysis revealed that 20 per cent of managers had high talent, 50 per cent were of average talent and 30 per cent of low talent, the profit growth of the groups being as follows:

High talent	plus	37%
Average talent	plus	4%
Low talent	minus	7.6%

The implications are that the talent-led company carefully seeds its candidates for redundancy, their decision of who can go being based on the level of talent they posess.

Equally, is it not conceivable that a company's ability to weather the current recession lies in its own hands and in the short, medium and long term, survival is dependent upon its ability to recruit and retain talent?

The significance of these results is not only in the effect on the profitability of the company but also in its impact on day to day operational management.

Conventional wisdom would suggest that line management devotes the majority of its time to the poor performers in an attempt to rescue them. These results turn that philosophy on its head in that quantum leaps in performance are achieved by devoting the majority of our time to our best performers.

That comment will generate a shock wave for a whole generation of managers. A shock wave because conventional wisdom requires them to devote the majority of their time to saving people or situations. Such managers want to spend their time changing people, hopefully for the better, concentrate on attempting to solve problems or improving marginal processes in order to achieve results. As Jack Falvey argues[2] 'What's wrong with the idea of managing those people or processes that are already working well? That is the area of management that produces most results consistently. Why must managers constantly work in areas of low percentage returns, trying to turn situations around'. The results of our survey comparing our top talented managers with the low talented group support that contention. Of course as managers we can change people, but it's only in the minority of situations that the results justify the time investment we have made. Equally, doesn't our day to day experience confirm that when we have invested substantial time and effort into changing people the effect has been short-lived, with most reverting back to type after a matter of days or weeks.

A further advantage in our company has been the reduction in labour turnover of pub managers which over the last three years has been reduced from 25 per cent to 20 per cent and is currently 15 per cent.

We have also used structured interviews for the selection of bar and restaurant staff. In an industry where high labour turnover is the norm (average of the industry in 1990 was 250 per cent), turnover within Joshua Tetley has steadily declined from 148 per cent to 97 per cent. While this is still high compared to other employment groups, it illustrates a considerable improvement.

An interesting comment that is frequently made by managers well experienced in the use of structured interviews, is that any stereotype preconceptions one may have had regarding an individual's sex, race or physical appearance are quickly disabused since the whole focus of the system is on the individual's talent profile. It's revealing to listen to managers discussing the relative merits of candidates; in the structured interview situation the debate centres very much on the individual's talent profile. In other interview systems, particularly the conventional face to face interview, the final choice is very often influenced by such subjective factors as appearance, sex, interview style, and so on.

It is certainly not unusual for companies that use structured interviews to evidence an increase in the ratio of women to men employed and in the number of women promoted or included in the management development programme.

As one example, during the mid 1980s 30 per cent of the Allied Breweries graduate intake was female. Since structured interviews have been used, the number of female graduates recruited has increased to 54 per cent. In Joshua Tetley within the sales and marketing functions the number of women employed in management during the early 1980s was 5 per cent. From the introduction of structured interviews in 1986 the number has increased to 20 per cent today.

COLONEL SAUNDERS – IT'S FINGER LICKIN' GOOD

Research studies into the effectiveness of structured interviews and the relationship between talent and profitability are very revealing. Harman Management are the largest franchisee of Kentucky Fried Chicken in the USA. Operating some 250 units they have been using structured interviews for the last 20 years.

In a study conducted in 1984, they determined that managers identified as 'highly' recommended on the interview achieved sales 9.5 per cent higher than those who did not meet the success criteria. At that time this equated to a $9,500,000 increase in volume.

In another Harman's human resource study, the ticket average of the 'highly' recommended group and those who did not meet the success criteria were compared, as well as the number of customers served per hour during peak periods. The 'highly' recommended group had a ticket average of $7.01 compared to those who did not meet the success criteria of $6.25; a difference of 76 cents per customer. The 'highly' recommended group served 6 more customers per hour on the average giving:

Management group	Customers
Highly recommended	$36 \times \$7.01 = \$252$ per hour
Did not meet success criteria	$30 \times \$6.25 = \$187.50$ per hour

4 peak hours per day × $64.50 per hour = $258.00 per day

or

$94,000 volume difference for each store per year.

A further feature of the use of structured interviews is, as already described, the effect on reducing labour turnover. Commenting on this point Einor W Bergstedt, President of Harman Management corporation says 'The low turnover rate of management at Harman's has saved literally thousands of dollars'. Harman's has averaged 19 per cent labour turnover in the last 10 years at store management level compared with the industry average of 50 per cent turnover. At a cost of approximately $10,000 per manager lost, the cost to the organisation is:

		Turnover		Managers	Cost
Harman's	1 year – 400 managers	19%	=	76	$760,000
Industry average	1 year – 400 managers	50%	=	200	$2,000,000

So in one year, the cost saving to Harman's is $1,240,000 and this is only at the management level. To extend this to front line workers the numbers are different but the result is the same tremendous cost savings just on labour turnover. Harman's co-worker turnover rate of 125 per cent may seem high but is excellent compared with the 400 per cent average for the American quick service industry. The saving per unit is $22,000, making a saving over 250 units of $5,500,000.

FURTHER EVIDENCE – AIRLINE PERFORMANCE

Further examples of the impact on company performance are available from documented validity studies in the airline industry. The definition 'low' refers to employees who did not meet the success criteria and 'high' to those employees who were highly recommended for employment as a consequence of successfully completing the appropriate structured interview (see Figures 2.4 and 2.5 on pages 50 and 51).

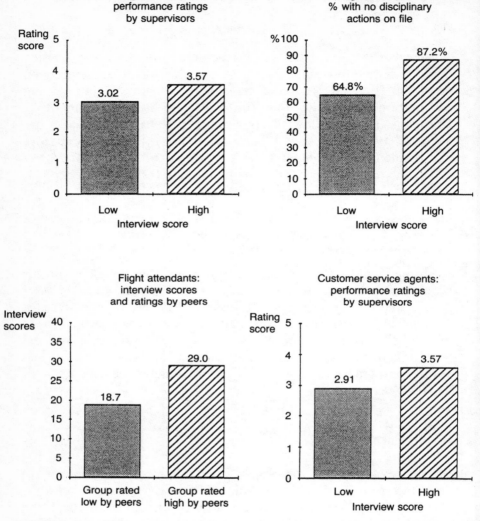

Figure 2.4 Documented validity studies of airlines – flight attendants

THE BOTTOM LINE IS DRIVEN BY FRONT LINE TROOPS

As the service sector becomes an increasingly important part of Western economies, service companies that wish to survive the 1990s can no longer treat staff as an expendable commodity or select and recruit employees on the basis that they applied for the vacancy and 'they were warm'. The reality is that in service organisations

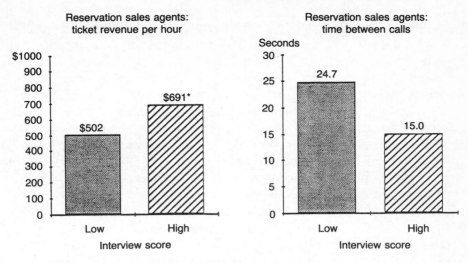

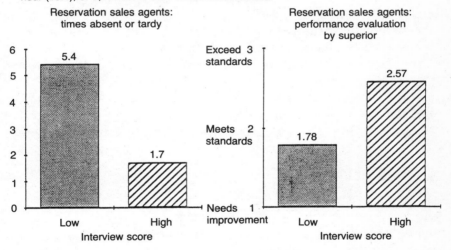

Figure 2.5 Documented validity studies of airlines – reservation sales agents

the bottom line is driven by front of house staff. The failure of most companies to recognise this essential truth means that they continue to sow the seeds of their own destruction by underinvesting in their front line troops. This point is graphically described by Leonard Schlesinger and James Heskett.[3] Their central thesis is that conventionally based service companies, although having been successful over the last 40 years or so, are becoming obsolete in that 'they follow an industrial model based largely on the principles of traditional mass production manufacturing. Attracting and maintaining today's customers demands a fundamentally new approach'. This new approach, they argue, means discarding the old service model, as typified by McDonald's, which 'puts the people who deliver to the customer last', and replacing it with the new service model which 'puts front line workers first and designs the business systems around them'. Examples of the new service model include Fairfield Inn, Dayton Hudson and Taco-Bell, companies which have made 'service delivery the centrepiece of their competitive strategy'.

A key feature of that strategy for Taco-Bell has been the selection of front line staff who have a talent for customer service. As Schlesinger and Heskett describe, Taco-Bell 'uses a selection system that is designed to elicit prospective employee values and attitudes towards responsibility, team work, and other **life themes** that have been shown to correlate with successful service work', in short, structured interviews. But the network of 'new service model' companies is more widespread than Schlesinger and Heskett envisaged. Among a range of companies in the USA investing in their front line troops through imaginative training and development, focusing their activities through reward and recognition and using structured interviews for selection are the Walt Disney Corporation, American Woodmart, Harman Management, Ritz Carlton Hotels and Cancer Treatment Centres of America. In the UK the list includes Allied Breweries, Standard Life, Holmes and Marchant, Motorola, Greenalls Inns and Inter-Continental Hotels.

SALESPEOPLE THAT SELL

As we come to the end of this section it is appropriate that we should reference and acknowledge the work of Dr William E Hall, who since 1960 has devoted his life to the development of structured interviews and to refining their use for predicting the potential of people for a wide range of occupations. One area of specific interest has been the study of outstanding salespeople in the USA,[4] and during the last 25 years or so both he, and his wife Susan, have interviewed over 10,000 individuals. In their research they have identified five prime themes that outstanding salespeople possess namely, ego drive, intelligence, focus, relationship and persuasion. Since it's a fact of life that nothing happens in organisations until someone buys something, the role of sales personnel in ensuring the continued existence and prosperity of the enterprise is of fundamental importance. It therefore follows that we need to understand these themes more fully if we are to ensure that we select salespersons who have the capacity to be truly outstanding. So let us examine in more detail the five themes that Dr Hall has identified.

Ego drive

Most students of human personality agree in general that every human being believes he or she has the potential to achieve success in some form of human endeavour. By success, we mean that an individual can perform something better than the average person which will attract attention and give them satisfaction when performing this activity.

We can therefore define ego drive as 'the desire on the part of the individual to express one's potential to perform an activity'. Such individuals have a continuous need to improve on every performance, this improvement enhancing their feeling of self-worth.

While manifestations of a high ego drive are many and various, William and Susan Hall have identified three key indicators. Firstly, outstanding salespeople determine the level of their performance by comparison with the performance of others. When asked how important it was to excel, the most common response was that 'it is very important' or 'I can't think of anything more important' or 'if you can't be first or at least strive to be the top guy, you shouldn't even try'. This set of responses is in marked contrast to the individual with a low level of competitiveness who will often respond: 'I have learned to lose' or 'if you can't lose you shouldn't play the game'.

Secondly, they need recognition from others to mark their achievements. If they do not receive appropriate acknowledgement when it is merited they 'feel hurt and let down'. Continued lack of recognition for their efforts will invariably lead to their leaving the organisation.

Thirdly, individuals who early on in life recognize a sense of responsibility tend to have a stronger ego drive. Parental attention was normally very important, irrespective of whether it was given in a warm or harsh fashion. However, strict discipline to support a family value normally develops a standard of behaviour that becomes important in assuming responsibility.

Intelligence

The second key theme identified was intelligence. While intelligence has several definitions, in the study of salespeople it has three components: the constant desire to search for information, the ability to discriminate and the ability to adapt to new situations. The indicators of intelligence in sales personnel are many and various and include the search for more knowledge about what they are doing and want to do. Every great salesperson admits that you need to have considerable technical competence to meet the needs of the client, but a much less understood fact is that outstanding salespeople seek out other outstanding performers to exchange ideas, sales techniques and compare track records. This desire for information seems to be a lifelong ambition and satisfies the need to be a person of significance.

Such people are equally able to discriminate and are sensitive to differences between ideas and people. They enjoy variations and have a particular ability to determine the 'just noticeable differences', constantly asking 'which' and 'what' in their evaluations to determine the importance of such differences.

The ability to adapt creatively to new situations is equally important, with the good salesperson not only being aware of the changes he must make to adapt to clients, but equally ensuring that the change has worked.

When an intelligent person has time, he or she pursues hobbies and interests that challenge the intellect, such as bridge, chess or reading, frequently taking notes on what they read. Outstanding salespeople equally have the habit of committing important things to paper, they keep records of successes and collect ideas or techniques that, to them, spell improvement.

Focus

As our lifetime experiences have taught us 'People can be divided into four groups: those who make things happen, those who think they make things happen, those who watch things happen and those who do not know that anything has happened'.

Dr Hall defines focus as 'one's ability to summon all of our energy and channel it down a course of action to make things happen'. The ingredients of this theme include a high energy level, the realisation of the value of time and effort expenditure, the ability to set meaningful goals, effectively organize and use time, realistically evaluate results and focus on the future. These are characteristics that all outstanding salespeople possess.

One interesting conclusion from the studies is that one's energy level is an 'inherent characteristic'. The research equally showed that the hyperactivity which some mothers and teachers deplore and attempt to constrain, is a common factor among people who later in life become outstanding.

Relationship

The fourth key theme is relationship, defined as the 'response one makes to the existence of another person'. If the recipient of our relating effort benefits from our relationship we say the relationship is a good one.

The ability of good salespeople to build sound, productive relationships with clients and colleagues is a key factor in determining success. Hardly surprising is the fact that they are people-orientated individuals who are stimulated by others, and generally belong to social, professional and community organisations.

One of the most interesting characteristics of the 'natural salesperson' is the ability to build an almost instant rapport with strangers in any situation. A discriminating question for identifying people with this skill is to ask them whether when they are at a social gathering they like to spend more time with friends or with strangers. Almost invariably the 'natural salesperson' recognizes that they spend more time with strangers.

Dr Hall is the first to admit that relationship is not a simple or easy way to influence people favourably. In his experience and study of relationship he has found that the most effective relationships were based on what he calls 'The Law of Parsimony', which states, 'In a life span, a talented, dedicated individual can initiate and develop only a finite number of helpful relationships; so, in parsimony, he should select the people with whom he builds the most significant relationships.' This does not necessarily mean he builds relationships with people who need it the most.

Persuasion

The fifth and final key theme is persuasion, defined as the 'development of an especial kind of relationship which established trust so someone can convince another to do something they have not thought of doing or to which they had shown some resistance'. The art of persuasion is a blend of certain skills which includes feelings of sensitivity towards another person, the skill in establishing wants, values and interests of the potential buyer, the ability to recognize when to seek to close the sale, and, last but not least, the skill to follow up on client satisfaction and benefit from the sale. Top performing salespeople have those skills in abundance and in particular instinctively understand that establishing trust is the key to any sale.

Based on the understanding of salespeople through structured interviews Dr Hall has developed a strategy for 'productive performance' which has enabled many salespeople to double or quadruple their sales.

As our domestic and international markets are becoming even more competitive, understanding the talents and key characteristics of our top performing sales personnel and seeking to recruit more of them will be of paramount importance to our future survival.

As we have demonstrated the first component in the talent equation is to commit the organisation to the single minded objective of only recruiting talent. We then need to study and understand our top performers and ensure that our selection systems are able to identify similar talented individuals. The pay off is for real.

SUMMARY

In this chapter we have concluded that:

- The main driving force behind Joshua Tetley's wish to make significant change in its selection methods, was the strategic decision to alter its business focus from product oriented to customer service driven. Furthermore, there was a clear appreciation that the ability to deliver that strategy was dependent upon the quality of the people recruited, particularly those at the customer interface. This is a strategy capable of wider application.

- The process of structured interviews involved Joshua Tetley in establishing for one occupational group 18 themes that were predictive of an individual's ability to be successful in pub management. Examples were given of the types of questions that tapped into a number of themes, together with the elements to listen for in response to those questions. As will be appreciated, a number of those themes will be relevant to other occupational groups but the questions asked and the responses listened for may vary widely.

- Effective operation of structured interviews with constant emphasis on talent requires organizations to change their advertising style and format. A number of examples of themed advertisements together with details of their relative effectiveness have been illustrated.

- In the talent led organization all members of operational management are involved in identifying talent both within and outside the company. Equally they never stop resourcing talent, when they are over-establishment they create a talent bank thereby avoiding the feast to famine syndrome of the conventional approach to recruitment.

- The validated studies of the impact of talented individuals recruited through structured interviews demonstrated a considerable improvement in profitability, growth and people performance.

- In recruiting individuals who have the capacity to add incremental growth to our activities we need to appreciate that time is the variable, talent the constant.

REFERENCES

1 Maynard, J (1982) *Restaurants and Institutions* Gahners Publishing Co, Illinois, USA, January.
2 Falvey, J (1981) The Benefits of Working With the Best Workers', *The Wall Street Journal*, May 11.
3 Schlesinger, L S and Heskett, J L (1991) 'The Service-Driven Service Company', *Harvard Business Review*, September/October.
4 Hall, William E and Hall, Susan R (1986) *The Salesperson*, Unpublished Manuscript.

THE SIX ISSUES FOR THE BOARD AGENDA

1. Identify the top 10 per cent performing employees in the company and calculate the contribution they make to the bottom line. Then assess the impact on company performance if we were to double that number by recruiting similarly talented individuals.

2. Review the company's current selection methods and pose the question whether they produce candidates that match the best operators in that occupational group.

3. Regularly monitor the predictions of our selection system against actual job performance.

4. Review our recruitment advertising and establish to what degree it screens talent in as well as screening non-talent out.

5. Encourage our management team to become the organization's talent spotters, track their performance in identifying talent both within and outside the organization and recognize those that are our natural talent spotters.

6. Never stop recruiting, when we are over-establishment, establish a talent bank.

► PART 2 ◄

Using Reward as the Lubricant for Success

3

Influences on Reward – from the Engineer to the Grocer's Daughter

Now that we have become a company that is committed to recruiting talent, the next component in our talent equation is to become an organization that has a genuine desire and ability to reward and recognize. Reward and recognize not just high performance, but reward it in a way that maximizes both individual and group contribution to the organization.

Despite the growth over the last five years in imaginative pay-for-performance schemes, the vast majority have been restricted to the ranks of management, with company chairmen and their senior executives being the main beneficiaries. That there has been a reluctance to cascade such schemes through the organization is understandable. Since the end of the First World War a whole series of philosophies have been advanced on how companies can motivate people at work. Few, if any, having fulfilled the expectations raised by their proponents.

Accordingly management's attitude to reward over the last 70 years has been influenced by a number of schools of thought. Their advocates and proponents attract a diverse group of individuals and professions ranging from the engineer, academic, guru, politician, social scientist, trade unionist and finally the grocer's daughter. A range of individuals who, while they would never have agreed to sit down to dinner together, have all had a considerable impact on our attitudes and perceptions to reward. This impact we need to understand and be discriminatory about, if we are genuinely to create an organization that understands the power of reward and recognition.

HISTORICAL INFLUENCES

The engineer – F W Taylor

The leading exponent of 'scientific management', F W Taylor was responsible for popularizing this technique for regulating performance and pay at work through time and motion study, payment by results schemes and bonus schemes based on industrial engineering principles.[1]

While such schemes, even today, have their advocates, their history is very much a chequered one, the essential problem being that, despite how much attention is paid to the design and construction of such schemes, the recipients will always find a way of circumventing and exploiting the control systems. Examples of individuals and teams artificially restricting their output levels during the observation period are commonplace. Despite the efforts of the industrial engineering function to make allowance for this factor, the standards and work rate they proposed were then normally the subject of collective bargaining which further diluted those standards.

Minor changes in product design, working practices and supplier requirements which impacted on bonus or piece rate earnings became setpiece battlegrounds as the shop steward movement sought either to protect earnings or to exploit deficiencies. Schemes that were designed to substitute reward for the frustration of having to submit daily to boring, repetitive jobs in reality produced their own frustrations and conflict.

That the shop steward movement exploited such inherent conflict is hardly surprising nor is the fact that, during the height of the popularity of piece rate working and its many derivatives, we saw a corresponding growth in the influence and number of shop stewards.

Given that experience, it was hardly surprising that management should have become disillusioned with the concepts of measurement and incentives. But have we 'thrown the baby out with the bath water?'

The academic – Frederick Herzberg

The academic in the guise of Frederick Herzberg has been a major influence on managements attitude to the reward and motivation of people at work. His theory on motivation[2] being derived from research into the factors which cause satisfaction or dissatisfaction in the workplace.

Herzberg's theory is based on the view that quite different sets of factors are responsible for individuals feeling satisfied or dissatisfied at work. Those which cause dissatisfaction, Herzberg describes as hygiene factors – those elements which form the work environment but are not part of the job itself. Examples include job security, wage or salary, working conditions, health and safety policies, and so on; the central thrust of his theory being that if these elements are missing or insufficient regard is paid to them, employees will get dissatisfied. But once they are adequate, making them better will not cause positive satisfaction.

In contrast, those elements which cause positive satisfaction, described as motivators, are 'those things which derive from the actual jobs that people do'. Examples include personal growth, increased responsibility and opportunities for greater decision making, and recognition for achievement – real improvement in the motivation of employees deriving from enriching individuals' jobs so that they can experience the daily effect of these motivators.

Herzberg's theory generated a culture shock for a whole generation of British management who, while wedded to a belief in pay and incentives as the prime tool in motivating employees, had become increasingly disenchanted with payment by results systems and the like. The new horizons that Herzberg's work opened were further compounded by a number of studies and surveys that had revealed that employees ranked pay way down the list of factors that created job satisfaction.

The result was that incentive and performance pay systems were dismantled and replaced by job enrichment programmes. In doing so, companies had missed one of the essential elements of Herzberg's work in that recognition is a positive motivator and positive recognition can be derived from the application of soundly based financial incentives.

The guru – Peter Drucker

Running alongside job enrichment programmes was the growth of management by objectives, a concept popularized by one of the most eminent of management gurus, Peter Drucker.

Essentially, the MBO system involves the identification of the key result areas for each job in the organization and the joint specification between the job holder and his manager of explicit targets to be achieved in those areas over the ensuing year. Progress meetings are held with subordinates during the year to review performance against the specified targets and by a process of coaching and counselling enable the individual to meet the set goals.

In essence, few would disagree with the principle of MBO with its central focus of joint goal setting and helping subordinates achieve those goals through a process of coaching and counselling. In practice, however, even the most committed adherents encounter the problem of ensuring that quantifiable targets are set, with far too many examples of generalized statements, with no specific measurable outcomes, being paraded as objectives.

The politician

The politician wears the colours of both major UK parties since they have equally directly interfered with the ability of organizations to determine the level at which it rewards its employees, the basic proposition being that, in advanced economies where inflation, employment, growth and the balance of payments have a significant influence on government policy and objectives, prices and pay cannot be determined for long by the free play of market forces.

As Incomes Data Services Study 148 outlines, since the end of the Second World War five major institutions have been established to monitor or control pay and prices in the UK:

1. Council On Prices, Productivity and Incomes (1956);
2. The National Incomes Commission (1961);
3. The National Board of Prices and Incomes (1967);
4. The Pay Board (1973);
5. Ultimately, the Department of Employment and the Price Commission.

During the period 1964 to 1979, a combination of 'pay pauses and thaws' meant that employers and employed alike were subjected to some 12 pay policies. They came in every shape and variety,[3] ranging from part percentage, part flat rate (eg, £1 plus 4 per cent); flat rate payment (eg, £6 per week for all); and percentage increase plus index linking to Retail Price Index (eg, 7 per cent plus up 40p for every 1 per cent rise over 7 per cent in the October 1973 RPI).

As will have been noted, from time to time they also prescribed the minimum and maximum payments employees could receive from the application of percentage limits and one policy even provided that anyone earning over £8500 per annum would receive no increase at all.

The effect of that policy continues to be felt, even today, in that anyone who was earning £8500 or more and was about to retire had their final salary artificially restricted and, as a consequence, their final pension was depressed.

It would not be unkind to suggest that the construction of these policies owed more to political expediency and dogma, the inventiveness of the Civil Service and 'horse trading' with the TUC, than it did to the ability of employers to pay or their need to focus reward in different ways.

The trade unionist – Mr Solemn Binding

The trade unionist, as represented by the General Secretaries, of the top six unions in the UK, was actively courted by all governments, irrespective of their political persuasion, as they sought to persuade them to, at best, support their incomes policies and, at worst, not oppose them.

A whole range of devices were used, ranging from introducing legislation for extending individual rights in employment, price control, influencing the content of the pay policies themselves, and so on. While this period in British history has been parodied as the time of 'beer and sandwiches at Number 10', its effects in raising to an all-time high the status and influence of the TUC General Council translated itself throughout the ranks of the trade union movement to the shop floor and management alike.

Management by appeasement became widespread, not simply in terms of the size of wage and salary increases during the periods of 'free collective bargaining' but in the acceptance and institutionalization of restrictive practices.

The right of management to manage also came under pressure, with calls from politicians, trade unions, and those executives who wished to be seen as 'enlightened', for the practices of communication and consultation to become codified and extended into some form of industrial democracy modelled on European institutions. It is interesting to recall that, during the mid 1970s, we came close to having legislation on industrial democracy that would have established two-tier company boards composed in part of elected trade union officials.

The social scientist

Throughout the 1960s, and up to the mid 1970s, management and politicians were increasingly susceptible to the influence of the academic fraternity, particularly the Oxford School of industrial relations. A key influence on industrial relations during that period was the Royal Commission on Trade Unions and Employers Associations. In addition to the report of the Commission itself, probably one of its more influential research papers on management thinking was Alan Fox's research paper on 'Industrial Sociology and Industrial Relations'.[4] In his incisive paper he constructs a frame of reference through which the problems of industrial relations can both be analyzed and solutions constructed.

The answer to the question 'what sort of organization is the industrial enterprise?' he suggests 'depends on whether we view it as a unitary or pluralistic structure'.

Viewing the industrial enterprise as a unitary system, he suggests, results in our perceiving organizations as having 'one source of authority and one focus of loyalty'. The analogy of the professional sports team was used to describe organizations with the necessary components of everyone 'striving jointly towards a common objective, each pulling his weight to the best of his ability'.

In this description of organizational life there are 'no oppositionary groups or factions and, therefore, no rival leaders within the team. Nor are there any outside it.' The loyalty that is expected of those that are led is reciprocated by their leaders, with morale and success being closely connected and resting heavily on 'personal relationships'. 'The cliches of this ideology' he suggests, are only too familiar, being embodied in such phrases as: all on the same side; all in one company; all in the same boat, and so on.

In contrast, Fox argues that we have to see the organization as a

plural society containing many related but separate interests and objectives which must be maintained in some kind of equilibrium. In place of a corporate unity reflected in a single focus of authority, we have to accept the existence of rival sources of leadership and loyalty and attachment.

He goes on to say that the demands and claims on an organization and its managers are many and far-reaching. Competing pressures of attempting to satisfy the claims of employees, shareholders, consumers and government and maintaining domestic and international competitiveness, are commonplace. As a consequence he argues 'management must maintain at least a necessary minimum level of concern with all these claimants and cannot, therefore, govern entirely in the interests of any of them'. The result is that 'by the very nature of its function, management must sometimes act against the interests of workpeople as they see them, and this is incompatible with the concept of common purpose'.

Fox, accordingly, concludes that the pluralistic framework is a more accurate representation of organizational life and, as a consequence 'conflict is endemic to industrial organizations'.

The impact on industrial relations

While few seasoned practitioners would argue with Alan Fox's analysis, the way in which it was interpreted and applied gave rise to concern. In many companies, having accepted the 'conflict theory' they sought to channel that potential conflict into constructive ends by institutionalizing relations with the trade unions.

Company-wide collective bargaining procedures and consultative systems became commonplace together with employers enforcing trade union membership on employees through pre- or post-entry closed shops, directing all communications with employees through the shop stewards network and being successfully challenged when they did not.

Collectivism became the norm, with the inevitable subordination of individualism and decline in the ability of middle management and supervision to manage effectively. It was hardly surprising, therefore, that during the 1970s the personnel function was characterized as the fire-fighting department, being good at handling conflict.

While the promotion of good industrial relations will always be an essential part of the personnel department's activities, the 1970s were a lost decade for personnel in that the concentration on handling conflict meant they had neither the time nor the resources to play a constructive role in increasing company profits through the maximization of the abilities and talents of the organization's human resources.

The grocer's daughter – Margaret Thatcher

Given that scenario of the 1960s and 1970s it was hardly surprising that the era of 'Thatcherism' with its emphasis on individualism, economic policies based on the application of market forces, removal or reduction of state subsidies, introduction of legislation to curb trade union activities and the use of the strike weapon, had a major effect on the attitude and perceptions of management throughout the UK.

On the shop floor the government's policy of pursuing economic measures that sacrificed the maintenance of high employment in exchange for trade union support in controlling inflation through pay policies, heralded a new sense of realism. No longer could the trade union activists rely on the unquestioning support of their members, militancy being exchanged for concern for job preservation.

That this change in government philosophy and management attitude would be subject to challenge by the trade unions was never in doubt. With the benefit of hindsight, the major areas of confrontation were all too easy to predict: car manufacturing, printing and coal mining being the front runners. All three industries typically had ingrained restrictive practices, were resistant to change and contained high levels of shop floor militancy. The watershed for each arrived as a consequence of major confrontation.

For the motor industry it was Longbridge, the arrival of Sir Michael Edwards and the dismissal of Derek Robinson the engineering trade union convenor.

For the print industry it was the introduction of new technology and the decision by Rupert Murdoch to dismiss the 5000 employees at News International and enforce its introduction by relocating to Wapping.

For the mining industry it was the total opposition by the National Union of Mineworkers through it's president, Arthur Scargill, to the closure of uneconomic pits. The miners' strike lasted from 1984 through to 1985 and resulted in over 26 million working days being lost. Not only was it the longest running large-scale strike in postwar British industrial history but it also involved levels of violence that were unprecedented. The pitched battle at Orgreave left a stain on the British trade union movement as a whole and the National Union of Mineworkers in particular.

If Lonrho was the 'unacceptable face of capitalism' then Orgreave was the unacceptable face of trade unionism. I make that comment, not from any political stance but simply as someone whose family has been in coal mining for three generations and who for the first nine years of my working life worked down the pit at Kingsbury Colliery in the Warwickshire coalfield.

The price paid by the individual participants and the UK as a whole was high, but it quickly led to a radical readjustment in the balance of power between the trade unions and employers. While management currently basks in the reflected glow of a stable industrial climate, the achievement of this situation says more about the former leader of the Conservative government than it does about the willingness of management to put its own house in order.

The fact that it took a woman to give British management its masculinity back is beyond question. That comment could be misconstrued as sexist but given the fact that the overriding majority of executives are male, it is a reflection of reality. Some will argue that the power pendulum has now swung too far in management's favour and, for the minority of companies that have taken advantage of that situation the lesson is that such force is met eventually by an equally powerful push in the opposite direction.

The net result of the Thatcher years is that the 'pluralistic' view of industrial life has been supplanted on most board room agendas by the 'unitary' approach.

One can ask at this stage whether, if we are to become an organization that genuinely wishes to reward and recognize talent, should we not consign to the dustbin of antiquity the historical grand masters and theories of reward management? The answer is an unequivocal no. The reason being that with the required degree of adaptation a number of their philosophies can be modified to meet today's requirements. Equally, understanding some of the key influences that have given rise to a number of current management issues is of assistance in analyzing the means whereby they can be resolved.

MEASUREMENT IMPROVES PERFORMANCE

In the earlier reference to the work of F W Taylor we evidenced the fact that disillusionment with scientific management had led to the abandonment in a large number of companies of measurement-based incentive and reward schemes. One consequence is that the power of positive measurement is one of the most underutilized management tools, with most measurement systems being used to detect the errors and the malfunctions of the organization.

When we wish to apportion blame, there is no shortage in the number of measuring tools at our disposal. But when we wish positively to measure performance the common complaint is that there is an absence of objective data.

This point was vividly brought home to me some time ago when talking to a group of supervisors about what measurement they would wish to introduce to reward industrial employees. The question was received in silence, despite several promptings, until one brave individual said 'the problem is that you use measurement to punish us'. We will not change that attitude until we understand and practice the concept of positive measurement.

A key component in developing that philosophy is the acceptance that measurement improves performance. Properly set targets and measurements motivate individuals not only to meet but also to exceed them. One key factor that separates the non-talented from the talent led organization is that in the latter the decision has already been taken that while profit is an important measure of the organization's performance it is not an end in itself. In particular they understand that profit is the consequence of a large number of actions and outcomes.

One consequence is that talent led organizations give more airtime to the non-financial measurements of the company in order to improve overall performance. Such measurements include customer satisfaction ratings, quality and delivery standards, labour turnover, talent profile of the organization and effectiveness of training and development. These measurements and the targets the company is aspiring to not only feature in the list of the company's key success factors but equally are the principle elements on which individual performance is rated.

The motivational effect of measurement is further and substantially enhanced when we apply the lubricant of reward to those key measurements.

PERFORMANCE REVIEWS – GETTING COMMITMENT

In our reference to management by objectives we evidenced some of the common problems encountered. In addition to these, in many companies, there is a lack of commitment to the process of coaching and counselling, the performance review very often being seen as just another management chore. This lack of commitment results in the MBO system being hijacked by the management development function with an attendant growth in the bureaucracy supporting the system. It is hardly surprising therefore that a considerable number of reviewing managers, and those they review, are dismissive of the whole process as yet another paperwork exercise.

A further effect of the 'disincentivization philosophy' was the stand taken by a number of leading proponents of MBO that no reward should be attached to the achievement of the specific goals and targets identified in the individual's key result areas, the view being that any discussions on financial reward would interfere with the counselling and coaching process.

These criticisms of the MBO system do not imply a lack of support for it. Properly used, it can be a most effective mechanism for focusing employees on the key business areas of the organization. In addition, effective coaching and counselling can be a powerful tool in building a sound relationship between the subordinate and his manager, providing, of course, that it is genuinely done and there is a sincere desire on the part of the reviewing manager to help the subordinate improve his performance.

Most of us will have experienced good and bad reviews, the best being when we have been reviewed by those who have a real talent for developing others – those special individuals who experience a real satisfaction in helping subordinates grow.

My own worst experience was as a young mining student being reviewed by my pit manager, a blunt Yorkshireman nearing retirement. His lack of interest I could just tolerate, but what unnerved me most was the constant flicking of his eyes to a notice he had displayed on his office wall which said:

Old age and cunning will beat youth and enthusiasm every time.

In fact, most of the common deficiencies can be remedied relatively easily. For example, formally requiring performance reviews to be conducted on at least a twice yearly basis will ensure that we get over the annual event syndrome. Reviewing subordinates' performance with the reviewing managers on a regular basis, outside the review system emphasizes the importance of the MBO system.

Further quality checks can be implemented by the managing director and his board reviewing a sample of the completed performance reviews. Equally, training can assist both the reviewee and reviewing manager to establish quantifiable objectives and the attendant measurement systems to monitor progress. Small points maybe, but all effective in reinjecting enthusiasm and reinforcing commitment to the performance review.

SHAKING OFF THE YOKE

Although statutory incomes policies were abandoned in 1979 by the then newly-elected Conservative government, this period has left an almost indelible stain on the perceptions of both management and employed alike on the subject of reward and pay.

First, the practice of annual pay review has become an established norm. That this is so is hardly surprising given that every pay policy from 1970 had a clause insisting on that time scale. As Incomes Data Services point out in IDS Study 148: 'for some reason the myth existed that yearly settlements were the norm'. Their further research (IDS Study 158) shows that, in fact, prior to that time the duration of settlements varied from six months to two years.

Second, the application, particularly of common percentage increases, has perpetuated the practice of the going rate, with employees assessing the acceptability of pay offers against such a norm rather than on the ability to pay argument. This concept is further reinforced every time a government minister or Bank of England spokesman talks about wage increases not exceeding x per cent. While their motives might be laudable in terms of the connection between inflation, international competitiveness and wage and salary increases, they reinforce the perception of the going rate.

Equally, to be even handed, if the CBI does genuinely believe that wage and salary increases should be determined by a company's ability to pay then that philosophy must equally apply in both good and bad times. It is not uncommon to hear company spokesmen telling employees and the community at large that, in recessionary times, it's the company's ability to pay that must decide the size of the wage or salary increase. But in good times, we are told increases must be kept in line with inflation.

The application of these double standards does nothing to enhance the credibility of the company in the eyes of its workforce, and are unacceptable to the talent led company.

TOP PAY – NEED OR GREED

Equally, such messages are blunted by the growing publicity on the levels at which a number of company top executives are remunerated, and in particular the level at which the top chief executives are rewarded (see Table 3.1).[5]

To put these figures into perspective, 12 years ago BOC's chief executive, Richard Giordano, was in the news as Britain's highest paid director earning the then princely sum of £271,000.[6]

It will, of course, be argued that the reason for the spectacular growth in the amount paid to a number of chief executives is that their reward is based on company performance and the schemes are fixed and monitored by a committee of non-executive directors. That answer merely begs two questions: Who invites the non-executive directors onto the Board and how soundly are such schemes based?

A further illustration of double standards during the current

Table 3.1 Remuneration of top executives

Directors	Company (financial year ending)	Pay £	Dividends £	Total Pay & Dividends £
David Sainsbury	J Sainsbury (3.91)	na	24,570,524	24,570,524
'Tiny' Rowland	Lonrho (9.90)	1,530,951	14,733,632	16,264,583
William Brown	Walsham Bros (12.89)	8,136,274	1,220,961	9,357,235
Paul Sykes	P Sykes Group (3.90)	6,854,000	na	6,854,000
Sir John Templeton	Templeton, Galbraith & Handberger (12.90)	560,835	6,020,841	6,581,676
Jack Dellal	Allied Commercial Holdings (3.90)	6,204,245	na	6,204,245
Ronald Hobson	National Parking Corporation (3.90)	294,948	3,718,373	4,013,321
David Wilson	Wilson Bowden (12.90)	304,508	3,563,853	3,868,361
Alan Sugar	Amstrad (6.90)	186,000	3,478,462	3,622,462
Lord Sainsbury of Preston Candover	J Sainsbury (3.91)	189,000	3,448,308	3,637,308
Paul Hamlyn	Reed Int. (5.91)	na	3,630,211	3,630,211
Sir Donald Gosling	National Parking Corporation (3.90)	283,204	3,089,413	3,272,617
Viscount Rothermere	Daily Mail and General Trust (9.90)	349,064	2,816,208	3,165,272
Maurice Hatter	IMO Precision Controls (3.90)	2,052,458	999,668	3,052,126
Trevor Hemmings	Scottish & Newcastle Breweries (4.90)	na	2,874,587	2,874,587

na = Information not available

recession has been the considerable hike in salaries of the chairmen of the newly privatized public utilities. While justification for these increases has been based on the going rate argument and the need to prevent the individuals from being seduced by offers from the national and international conglomerates, one is left to speculate why, if they were so marketable, have they remained in their present industries for so long?

To be even-handed, however, we need to point out that the phenomenon of grossly inflated salary increases is not just restricted to the newly privatized public utilities. According to a recent survey[7] British chief executives during the period 1984–89 received, after tax, pay increases of just under 100 per cent compared with an increase in inflation of 28 per cent over the same period. Furthermore, in terms of the earnings differential between the UK boardroom and the shop floor, it is estimated that the chief executive earns just over 30 times more than his average employee.

However, the problem is not confined to the UK, and as Graef Crystal points out[8] the situation is even more extreme in the USA with the chief executives of major American companies earning 160 times the pay of their average worker. To put those figures into perspective, the average Japanese chief executive earns only 16 times as much as the average blue collar worker.

For a generation whose attitude and approach to pay and motivation has been influenced by the work of Herzberg and Maslow, and the many subsequent studies which have continued to relegate pay down the list of factors that positively influence job performance, the spectre of chief executives pursuing ever larger and larger salaries confounds conventional wisdom. The real issue, of course, is how do we account for this phenomenon. Can we dismiss it as simply due to executive vanity where status in the business community is perhaps perceived as being governed by the size of the salary cheque? Alternatively, can we blame simple greed or the extreme manifestations of a free enterprise culture, or is there perhaps a more fundamental reason?

Is it not just conceivable that the behavioural scientists need to revisit the models they have constructed to illustrate what influences performance at work and the relative impact those factors have in regard to economic well-being, age, class, occupational group, and so on, to establish whether at chairman/chief executive level a totally different value system operates from that influencing the behaviour of the rest of us in the managerial pile.

Is it not just possible that, having reached the pinnacle of the organization, those elements related to job satisfaction which motivate their subordinates no longer have the same appeal and, accordingly, money – the universal, if crude method of apportioning value – becomes the substitute?

Or, on mature reflection, do we disregard the views of the social scientists and instead rely on the wise judgement of John Kenneth Galbraith who said 'The salary of the chief executive of the large corporation is not a market award for achievement. It is frequently in the nature of a warm personal gesture by the individual to himself'?

I must emphasize that the key argument advanced in this section is not that we shouldn't address ourselves to the market forces arguments, or have imaginative pay for results systems, (the reverse, in fact, being the case) but why should such schemes be reserved almost wholly for the main board and their senior executives? In talent led organizations the chief executive and his board lead by example.

COLLECTIVISM AND THE UNIONS

A further legacy of the prescriptive nature of pay policies with upper and lower limits and, in some years, an across-the-board flat rate increase, was that any innovation in the personnel function towards employee reward systems 'died on the vine'.

How ingrained the bureaucratic approach to pay and reward became, is illustrated by the number of company-wide bargaining units or, in the public sector, the number of industry-wide agreements still in existence. Part of the answer for their continuation lies at the door of the trade unions who have, in the main, opposed the decentralization of collective bargaining. That such decentralization has been achieved in a number of companies and industries is a testament to management's determination.

The reason for trade union opposition is simple: company- and industry-wide agreements give them a power base in terms of controlling levels of pay and maintaining membership. Decentralizing collective bargaining takes away from them the opportunity of calling out a large section of their membership in advancing pay claims.

But the worst problem left over from the days of pay policies as typified by the across-the-board flat rate increase is that it reinforced the attitude that everyone should be treated equally. That thread of collectivism is an essential part of the psyche of the British trade union movement and its activists. It is one that will condemn the movement to continuing loss of membership as those it seeks to represent become more attracted to the benefits of an enterprise culture. A seed corn change is required, one that accepts that you can be compassionate to the less able while, at the same time, pursuing reward policies that recognize that those who perform the most effectively should receive the most. There is, after all, more injustice created by seeking to treat the indolent in the same way as the industrious. Policies of equal misery for all have few real advocates, even on the shop floor, and in the talent led company we need to consistently confront such views.

SUMMARY

In this chapter we have concluded that:

- Establishing imaginative and aspirational reward and recognition programmes is an essential component in maximizing the contribution that talent can have on company performance.

- We need to understand the seven principal influences on management's attitudes to reward, in order to have a better appreciation of some of the deep seated influences affecting our ability to respond creatively to these issues.

- The effects of these philosophies have been far reaching in their impact on many of our more commonly used systems for rewarding performance at work. They have equally been a powerful influence on our attitude to how we are rewarded irrespective of whether we operate at board level or on the shop floor.

- A key feature in developing reward systems that enhance individual and group performance is the acceptance of the philosophy that measurement improves performance.

- In the talent led company there is a clear understanding that in establishing appropriate measurements profit is not an end in itself but the result of a large number of actions and outcomes. Accordingly such measurements as customer service standards, staff turnover or quality standards are recognized as being factors which generate reward.

REFERENCES

1 Taylor, F W (1947) *The Principles of Scientific Management*, Harper, New York.
2 Herzberg, F, Mausner, B and Synderman, B (1957) *The Motivation to Work*, John Wiley, New York.
3 Brewster, C (1984) *Understanding Industrial Relations*, Pan, London.
4 Fox, A (1966) Industrial Psychology and Industrial Relations Research Paper No 3, Royal Commission on Trade Unions and Employers Associations, HMSO, London.
5 Labour Research, August 1991.
6 'Best-Paid Boards', (Inside Story), *Management Today*, June 1991.
7 'Top Pay – A 20 Year Perspective' (Sept 1991, no 127 pp 14–16) *IDS Top Pay Review*.
8 Crystal, G S (1992) *In Search Of Excess*, Norton, New York.

4

What Happens in Organizations is What we Reward

With the historical legacy already discussed, it's hardly surprising that management has shown an amazingly high level of disregard for the benefits of implanting into their organizations a philosophy of positive measurement and rewarding and recognizing success. It is however, a stance we adopt at our peril since one of the key requirements of talented individuals is to have their endeavours both recognized and rewarded. The absence of one or other of those commodities results in the individual either underperforming or leaving their organization.

The reluctance of companies to engage in positive reward and recognition that touches talented individuals at every level in the organization is, as we have said, partly due to history, but it equally has to be admitted that the unwillingness by a small number of managers to reward the excellence they cannot attain is also powerful. Perhaps Alistair McLean best summed up that part of human nature when he said 'base envy hates that excellence it cannot reach'.[1]

However, since the latter group are in a clear minority let us concentrate on convincing the organization that effectively constructed reward and recognition policies can make a difference to the company's performance, a substantial difference for the better.

GREAT PERFORMERS, GREAT PERFORMANCES

Perhaps the first step in that process is for us to understand that while we readily accept the breakthroughs in automation and information technology and embrace the fact that the frontiers of science will continue to be ever rolled back, less well understood is the fact that no one has yet prescribed the limits of human achievement. In terms of physical endurance, the world of sport offers the most regularly changing examples of how limits, once set, are not only met but exceeded. Equally, however, examples from the world of industry and commerce can be discovered.

A major British double glazing organization was recently considering the future of its north-east operation. Business levels had fallen to a level where the future of its depot in Stockton was under critical review. Conventional wisdom within the company believed the problem was due to a depressed local economy and a lack of brand image. That is, until they recruited Ray Moses as regional manager. The company required £20,000 a week sales as a break-even figure. Within a few weeks Ray's team was achieving sales of £40,000. Sales targets of £60,000 and £75,000 were progressively beaten and, recently, they were achieving sales of over £100,000 per week.

The company's managing director believes the total turnaround in performance was due to 'Ray's tremendous talent for selling and motivating his sales team and the major incentives the company offers when targets are beaten'.

Some three years ago the Tesco supermarket group, as part of its programme of increasing customer service, introduced a 'Mystery Shopper' programme. This involved independent shoppers visiting different stores and rating them on a range of key items, including friendliness of staff, range of product availability, speed of service, and so on. A total of 360 stores took part, with an average score of 70 per cent. The winner was the Stafford store with an incredible score of 91 per cent. Commenting on their success, Manager Ian Tann said 'Employing a talented team and having the desire to win were the key ingredients in coming top'.

But it's not only in large stores that the record breakers are to be discovered. Martin and Bernie Tremlett are licensees of the Original Oak, a well-known venue to spectators at Headingley cricket ground in Yorkshire. In an industry where real growth in profit is increasingly investment led, Martin and Bernie have increased their profit, by their own efforts, by 20 per cent year on year for the past five years. They consistently hit the number one spot in their company's sales league table and, last year, achieved sales of over £1,000,000. While many attributes have led to their success, for Martin and Bernie running the Original Oak was the realization of a lifetime's ambition. This, added to their high degree of competitiveness fuelled by the bonus system they operate under, and caring for customers, ensures that their success is not short term but for the long run.

Finally, the often told but frequently apocryphal story of the salesman who earns more than the company chairman. Well, we had to travel across the Atlantic to discover Mehdi Fakharzadeh, a sales representative with Metropolitan Life Assurance, whose commission earnings last year were in excess of $1,000,000 and grossed more than the chief executive of the company.

These examples may appear unique, but the fact of the matter is that they are simply representative of that rich vein of talent that lies within most companies. The tragedy is that, in far too many organizations, it lies undisturbed.

PUTTING 40 PER CENT MORE EFFORT ON THE BOTTOM LINE

That it does lie undisturbed was vividly brought home to me during a recruitment exercise in 1987. As part of the screening exercise, we asked 500 applicants to relate to us a time when they had received special recognition or reward. Fifty per cent related an instance at school or college when they had received an award for either scholastic or sporting achievements. Of the remainder, only five per cent were able to find an unprompted instance relating to work and yet in many instances they had been employed by the same company for 15 years or more.

The effects of not recognizing and rewarding talented performers goes right through to the bottom line of the organization. It is an indisputable fact that in most companies *we can demand at best up to 60 per cent of an individual's efforts – the remaining 40 per cent they give us*. The ability to promote and productively utilize that hidden 40 per cent makes the difference between an average and an excellent company.

Are we getting what we reward?

The key question for organizations, therefore, is how can we stimulate that undisturbed talent into action, stimulating it in such a way that individual and group efforts coincide with, and are supportive of, company goals and objectives. Part of the answer lies, first, in how we structure our reward systems and second, the approach we adopt in recognizing high performance either within or outside the formal reward system.

In terms of reviewing the effectiveness of our current payment systems, we have to appreciate the fact that the way in which we reward employees telegraphs up clear and visible indicators of those activities and behaviours the organization values and wishes to promote.

The reality, whether we are always conscious of it or not, is that *what happens in organizations is what we reward*. It is a salutary experience for most companies to review their current payment systems against that benchmark.

For example, service related progression through the salary range, while designed to be equitable and retain employees through rewarding long service, often produces, in practice, a very different mode of behaviour. If long service is the key to reward then what price risk taking or innovation? Why take the chance? Conformity and slavish adherence to the rules become the norm. If everyone is rewarded on the same basis, employees may end up asking themselves why they should perform at a higher level than the lowest common denominator.

Payment schemes which are related to volume and output focus attention on the amount produced with little regard being paid to quality. In such systems, quality becomes the sole prerogative of the quality control department – in other words, someone else's responsibility.

Basic rate payment systems with hours worked in addition to the standard week being paid at premium rates also have drawbacks. While being designed to give stability to earnings levels and provide greater control by management and supervision of hours actually worked, they often produce the reverse. Such systems can in practice actually encourage the amount of overtime worked, with earnings fluctuating in accordance with the individual's pay needs rather than production requirements. Even worse, it can encourage a silent conspiracy between supervisors and employees that co-operation is only obtained through the overtime rota. Time becomes the key motivator with efficiency and effectiveness being the victim.

Company-wide profit share schemes designed to promote greater acceptance of the profit motive and a climate of cooperating and working together often produce, at best, a neutral reaction. The reality is that large sections of the workforce can only influence profit at the margin. The major decisions that affect profit – pricing strategy, product design, innovation and investment decisions – being the prerogative of a small number of key decision makers.

This argument is not a denial of the fact that everyone can make a contribution to an organization's effectiveness and profitability; clearly the opposite is a matter of fact. It is simply that profit, as a key element in the reward system, can be inappropriate for a large number of those employed.

Share ownership

Share ownership schemes are often heralded as a prime tool in promoting behaviour and attitude change throughout the organization. Sir Peter Thompson, president of the National Freight Corporation, has long been a consistent advocate of the positive benefits of increased share ownership among employees. Commenting on the subject he says: 'The argument goes that, if the workforce can be persuaded to behave as if they own a problem, a service, or a product, their behaviour will change and from that change will flow better quality'.[2]

Other proponents would argue that, when individuals have a share holding in the company, they undergo a radical attitude change and become more committed to the long-term profitability growth of the company.

While few would argue with the sentiments underlining those basic propositions, the central question is, however, do share ownership schemes consistently produce that behaviour and long-term commitment to the organization? The reality for a large number of the workforce is that, first, the ability to translate their day to day activities into its effect on the organization's profit performance is difficult.

Second, the effort they put into their day to day jobs is immediate. In contrast, the effects of that effort on the company's profit performance can be up to 12 months away and can be diluted by the actions of their peer group and all the other factors that make up organizational life.

Third, they quickly appreciate that a company's total profit performance is directly affected by a whole series of factors outside their control – the general economic climate, interest rates, the activities of others in key decision-making roles – areas in which they can bring little influence to bear.

Fourth, they come to realize that the amount of stock they actually own is only a minute proportion of the total and that the real power in influencing the direction a company takes lies in the hands of the main board and the institutions.

Finally, while the argument that such schemes give individuals a stake in the long-term growth in share value is seductive, they quickly appreciate that share price in the short- and medium-term is governed more by national and international confidence and the vagaries of the stockmarket than company performance. And in the long term? Well, as Maynard Keynes said: 'in the long-term we're all dead', the net result being that large numbers of employees, having acquired shares, quickly dispose of them and take the profit.

It has to be admitted, however, that since most schemes are service related in terms of the eligibility to enter, and most stipulate a minimum period that shares have to be held, they are an effective way of retaining employees. But, do we wish to apply 'golden handcuffs' indiscriminately?

While many claims are made in support of share ownership schemes for employees, for example, as a means of enabling individuals to build up capital or focusing the activities of key executives, share option schemes are excellent. It is however, doubtful if they produce a seed corn change in the attitude of the workforce at large or generate for the long term the behavioural changes desired.

RELATING PAY TO PERFORMANCE – THE CRITICS

The emphasis I have placed on reward as a means of stimulating individuals to higher levels of performance is not of course without its critics. Since the early 1990s doubts have been expressed by a small number of academics and personnel practitioners particularly in the public sector, as to the effectiveness of performance related payment (PRP) schemes.

The principle objections raised in respect of PRP have included concerns that concentrating reward at individual level is very often detrimental to team work. Another is that the organization's business priorities and objectives can change during the year, resulting in either an individual's goals no longer being relevant or being changed frequently. Reviewing managers ratings can be artificially depressed to fit an organizational norm, or ratings can be affected by the 'blue eyed boy' syndrome.

It is not surprising that a number of employees raise objections to PRP in principle; certainly life for them was more comfortable under the service related progression schemes that regulated in most situations progress from the minimum to the maximum of the salary scale. This was a system where, unless there was a major dereliction of duty, the annual increment was guaranteed. The downside for aspiring individuals was that promotion either inside or outside the organization was virtually the only means of escape. Equally, the possibility of improving individual performance was handicapped by the perception that if we are all going to be rewarded the same, mediocrity Rules OK.

In terms of the practice of PRP a number of the criticisms raised can be overcome by improved scheme design, ensuring that individuals can, in particular, influence the key performance measurements and that they are relevant. While the level of individual ratings has to have regard to the overall performance of the organization, the introduction of artificial measures such as a normal distribution curve to scale down ratings will, quite rightly, be received with scepticism by those affected. On the question of the impact of PRP on teamwork, one of course accepts that a number of our activities are dependant on the actions of others, but equally, isn't it a matter of fact that not everyone in the group or team performs at the same level? This issue does not present any real hurdle to the reward sensitive organization. For them the question is resolved by payments being triggered by both team and individual effort. It should also be noted that in some organizations the impression is gained that the emphasis placed by a number of reviewing managers on team work and their inability to accurately reflect individual performance says a lot about their lack of ability to discriminate, and the absence of courage in wishing to do so. A number of commentators have said that it is regrettable that the whole area of PRP should have become so charged with emotion and in the public sector become so politicized. That this is so should, on mature reflection, come as no real surprise. There is after all in every organization a group for whom risk taking, competition and enterprise are an anathema. Where they are in the majority tall poppies never grow, they are cut down to size when they make themselves distinguishable from the pack.

It is a mentality born of the levellers of the 17th century when distinction of any description was abhorred. Team working for them is never seen as a group activity where individuals can flourish and experience achievements greater than the group norm, it is a place where individualism is sacrificed in pursuit of collectivism. It is a philosophy that in this century resulted in a maximum wage for professional footballers, continued for so long on the basis that if one or more of the team was paid more than the majority, team work would collapse – history has written its own epitaph on that viewpoint.

SUMMARY – THE FIVE PRINCIPLES OF REWARD

In summary, if reward systems are to be an effective method of motivating talent , we have to ensure that:

- We fully understand and are aware of the kind of behaviour we are seeking to promote, both in principle and in practice.

- Such behaviour is supportive of and in accord with our organizational goals.

- The key components of the reward or pay system have to be capable of being directly influenced by the actions of those to whom the schemes apply.

- The level of payment has to be aspirational. There is no fundamental logic, other than the inherent conservatism of a company, in having arbitrary cut-offs in the level of earnings that reward or incentive schemes generate.

- The frequency of payment has equally to be aspirational. The shorter the time gap between those performances that generate reward and the payment itself, the greater the corresponding effect on motivation.

Five principles to review your current reward systems against.

REFERENCES

1 MacLean, A (1969) *South By Java Head*, Collins, London.
2 Thompson, Sir Peter (1991) 'If People Share, They Care', *Management Today*, August.

5

Apply the Principles back at the Ranch

Since the majority of management books are written by either academics or consultants, a common complaint from management readers is that the theories advocated have not been tested on the anvil of day to day management, or that proponents have not been responsible or accountable for the application of the changes they have instigated.

This book avoids that complaint in that, in this section in particular, we explore some of the changes that have been brought about to the payment structures and reward systems in Joshua Tetley. We now focus our attention mainly on examples from within the company, to illustrate that the philosophy and ideas advocated in this book are capable of being successfully implemented in practice.

Implemented in practice in a company that has a tradition stretching back to 1822 with all that that entails in terms of the elements that promote common purpose and disharmony. Not for us the benefits of implementing change from the relative luxury of a 'green field site'.

APPLYING THE PRINCIPLES – JOSHUA TETLEY

Recognizing the relationship between company performance and how we reward employees, and building on the employee relations climate created by the Thatcher administration, Joshua Tetley undertook a radical review of its payment system throughout the organization.

The key objectives were to:

1. gain closer co-operation and commitment to change;
2. improve company performance and profitability;
3. provide a more equitable balance between individual performance and the level of individual reward;

4. increase the level of individual accountability and commitment;
5. retain out best performers.

The programme began in the mid 1980s and, to date, the following changes have been achieved through a combination of management determination, and employee and trade union cooperation.

The management structure

At the time of writing the structure within Joshua Tetley contains three levels of management:

1. Board directors;
2. Executive management;
3. Management.

The board comprises the chairman, who is managing director of the beer division of which Joshua Tetley is a regional, integrated trading company encompassing brewing, wholesaling and retailing activities. The company managing director is a member of the beer division board and reports to the managing director of the beer division. He, in turn, is supported on the Joshua Tetley board by six executive directors and two non-executive directors. The management structure is functionally focused, with each of the six executive directors heading up a key business area: production and distribution, retail operations, tenancy and leasehold, free trade, finance and personnel. Reporting to them are 30 executive managers who are responsible for the day to day operation of their departments, eg, head brewer, retail trade director, distribution manager, chief accountant etc. This group in turn, is supported by some 200 members of management who are responsible for managing sections of the business or providing technical or professional support to the line.

Rewarding managers – the background

The 200 members of management are encompassed within four grades, the grade for each job within the group being determined by a combination of factor analysis and pairs comparison. Each of the grades has a salary range with provision for annual movement from the minimum to the maximum of the grade. From the early 1970s through to 1984 progression through the salary range was service related with individuals achieving, subject to satisfactory performance, salary scale maximum in five years.

From what has already been discussed, the inadequacies of that situation will be only too apparent, the key problems being the inability to reward high performance, indications of the common denominator ruling and a lack of innovation and incentive.

A further problem was that, due to everyone achieving salary maximum over a relatively short period of time, the salary range from minimum to maximum of the grades was restricted to 20 per cent to avoid excessive paybill costs. This had the effect of not only restricting the company's ability to reward high performers but also limited it's ability to recruit in the marketplace, particularly at times of skill shortage in a particular discipline.

GETTING PERFORMANCE REVIEWS TO WORK

In 1984 after a series of negotiations with the union concerned, the decision was made to change the method by which managers progressed from the minimum to the maximum of the salary scale. In essence this involved converting from being a service-related to a performance-driven company.

The annual performance review from which a manager's performance is assessed against defined measurable objectives was agreed on as being the vehicle from which such assessment would be made. Five performance definitions were introduced:

- *Excellent* ('A' rating) – Consistently excellent performance. All qualitative and quantitative objectives met within time limits. Work standards are outstanding.

- *Very Good* ('B' rating) – Regularly performs to a high level. Work characterized by reliability, enthusiasm and innovation.

- *Good* ('C' rating) – Regularly meets all requirements of the job to a good standard. Objectives achieved with only limited support and direction from manager.

- *Fair* ('D' rating) – To achieve an adequate performance requires regular direction, support and guidance.

- *Inadequate* ('E' rating) – A less than acceptable level of performance. Individuals cannot be relied upon to meet objectives. Work characterized by errors, slowness and unreliability.

The performance related payment structure being as shown in Table 5.1.

An important by-product of the change from a service-related to a

Table 5.1 Joshua Tetley management payment structure

Grade	A £	B £	C £	D £	E £
5	1,262	947	631	316	0
6	1,432	1,074	716	358	0
7	1,588	1,191	794	397	0
8	1,830	1,373	915	458	0

performance-driven scheme was the impact it had on the performance review system. First, if reviewing managers were objectively to assess subordinate performance then the objectives set had to be both realistic and, as far as possible, quantifiable. This process was assisted by insisting that as far as possible all objectives were reduced to hard numbers and related, at least in part, to the company's key success factors.

Second, since reward was dependant upon the outcome, subordinates were unwilling to allow the review to be conducted in a less than professional manner or, equally, without adequate time for preparation by both parties. Attaching reward to the review process has probably done more to improve the quality of the performance review system than any other single measure and has certainly had more impact than all the training that was held on conducting effective performance reviews.

However, any system has its drawbacks and deficiencies. The principal problem in this case was that, in some areas, quantifiable and measurable objectives were less easy to arrive at, although converting the annual review into a twice yearly event and encouraging managers to review subordinates informally on a regular basis has been of some assistance in overcoming that particular problem. The second problem has been one of ensuring that there is some degree of correlation between the performance grades awarded and the actual performance of the department as a whole. The phenomenon of the review manager who sees all his subordinates as swans or all as geese is not rare.

Within the company, equity has been preserved by the executive committee reviewing all performance grades. This is certainly preferable to the practice in some organizations of applying arbitrary cash limits which can result in some departments receiving a cash allocation which is less than their performance warrants or others receiving more.

The third and probably the most significant problem was employees' expectations and perception on the ratings applied. A 'C' rating, which is given for 'good' performance over time becomes seen as 'coming up with the rations' and therefore the reward associated with it can act as a disincentive rather than a motivator – individuals describing their performance as 'only worth a C' rather than saying their performance was rated 'good'.

In an effort to get over that problem, the company has removed the A to E classification system and replaced it with a band of payments against each of the performance ratings of excellent to fair. In addition to addressing the problems outlined above, this will give reviewing managers more ownership of the scheme as they will have to decide the level of reward to be apportioned rather than having it directly pre-determined for them.

MOTIVATING MANAGERS

While I have described one of the problems associated with performance review schemes as being the difficulty in some areas of defining quantifiable and measurable objectives, there are obviously exceptions to this generalization. The interesting point being that the more one learns to set quantifiable and measurable objectives, the more exceptions to the non-measurement rule can be created. A useful yardstick is that if we cannot measure it why are we doing it?

In Joshua Tetley's retailing, tenancy and free trade operations hard, quantifiable data is readily available – sales turnover, operational expenses, gross and net profit, sales volume, account retention, new accounts gained, selling expenses, overdues and so on – it was, therefore, relatively easy to convert the performance related payment scheme in those areas into direct incentive schemes. The objectives of all three schemes were similar and were designed firstly to provide a direct financial incentive scheme which would act as a positive motivator for the generation of increased sales and profit. Secondly we needed to focus individual managers' attention and action on the key criteria influencing the development of an improved profit performance within his/her sphere of control. Each scheme normally contains up to a maximum of three elements as follows:

- Tenancy – total sales, negotiated rents, performance of amusement machines.

- Free trade – volume sales, accounts retained and gained, overdues.

- Retail – total takings and controllable profit performance against budget.

Each of the elements is weighted to reflect the relative contribution of each item to the company, each scheme being designed to generate up to around 40 per cent of basic salary. To enable progression through the salary structure, part of the incentive payment is used to fund salary progression up to the value of an 'excellent' rating, the residual amount being paid as a one-off lump sum.

The net result is that we have a group of managers who are highly motivated and whose areas of concentration and focus are in line with company objectives. A further advantage is that the results they achieve are, to a large extent, dependant upon the direction and support they give to those they manage out in the field of operations, a necessary consequence being that they have had to adopt a more supportive management style with their sales teams, pub managers or tenants.

I stated earlier that performance related payment schemes can be designed to reflect both team and individual needs. One such performance payment scheme applies to managers in our production, distribution and engineering departments. Originally managers in those areas were rewarded, over and above the annual negotiated increase, on the basis of their overall performance as assessed against the key result areas in the performance review system. However, following the successful introduction of the incentive based performance schemes for managers in the commercial trade related areas it was decided to investigate whether a payment scheme more directly related to actual bottom line performance could be introduced into a production dominated environment.

The decision to base the scheme on the three key measures of quality, service and cost effectiveness was quickly arrived at, as was the decision to generate payment by reference to performance improvement in each of the key target areas. The more challenging debate was whether the key performance levels should be targeted at individual, departmental or total functional level? The debate necessarily centred on the problem that on one hand in a process industry everyone contributes to quality, service and cost effectiveness, but on the other we all understand that some individuals contribute in a more effective way to the success of the team than others.

The solution arrived at was that performance against the three target areas was assessed over the function as a whole, the amount generated by improved performance being calculated globally. The concept of the 'global pot' recognized the total team work nature of this part of our business.

Then, in order to recognize individual contribution individual managers were assessed by the conventional PRP system as to their contribution during the year measured against the key result areas. The payment generated from PRP being the first charge against the 'global pot', the remainder being distributed as a one-off bonus to participating managers. This has proved an interesting example of the fact that, in the right circumstances, you do not have to choose between rewarding individuals or the team, you can do both.

CASCADING REWARD DOWN THE ORGANIZATION

It is a regrettable fact that in far too many organizations, incentives and reward initiatives stop at the management group when the real need is to cascade such schemes through the organization. If the idea that what happens in organizations is what you reward applies to executives and managers then it equally applies to everyone in the organization, irrespective of grade or job title.

Three examples from within Joshua Tetley where that philosophy has been successfully implemented are pub management, distribution, and production and engineering operatives.

REWARDING PUB MANAGERS – THE JOSHUA TETLEY EXPERIENCE

Active trade unionism and formalized collective bargaining for pub managers arrived late on the scene in the brewing industry, the major employers themselves actively supporting the establishment of the National Association of Licensed House Managers during the early part of 1970. The motives for this approach were not simply altruistic, more a growing concern at the possibility of the large industrial trade unions, who had a dominant membership amongst its brewery and distribution employees, extending their activities into the pubs. The potential net result being that one or two of the major trade unions could have achieved considerable bargaining muscle by controlling the membership in production, distribution and retailing.

Despite this late entry into the collective bargaining arena, the methods used to reward pub managers were reminiscent of the systems used in the traditional blue collar areas. In most companies, pub managers were rewarded by a salary related to a complex grading system and a bonus scheme related to either volume sales or profitability of the pub.

Grading structure

Joshua Tetley was no exception to the general rule and, up to the mid 1980s the pub manager salary structure comprised 10 grades, the grade of each pub being decided by an evaluation process involving 14 factors, regulated by a joint management and union panel.

Bonus schemes

Further financial incentives were provided through three bonus schemes:-

- Tier 1 – related to a non-discretionary bonus of 4 per cent of repair-free house net profit.

- Tier 2 – a further payment based on 10 per cent of additional real, repair-free house net profit based on a year on year comparison adjusted for inflation.

- Tier 3 – an incentive to increase barrels sold based on the average over the previous three years, which attracted a payment of £3 per barrel.

The problems and solutions

The problems inherent in such a payment structure are only too readily identifiable. First, a grading evaluation system which contains 14 assessment points, a number of which are open to subjective interpretation, contains all the ingredients for long wrangles and conflict.

Secondly, two of the key elements in maintaining the profitability of the pub – sales of drinks and food – were submerged in the list of 14 factors. It was hardly surprising that pub managers became out of focus, concentrating on attempting, *in extremis*, to obtain an upgrading through claiming that they have four open fires rather than three or the inconvenience of receiving beer deliveries at

7.00 am rather than 10.00 am and so on, instead of concentrating on increasing their sales.

Thirdly, the bonus structure was complex, with few of the managers really understanding how it operated. In particular, the value of Tier 1 bonus, which was 4 per cent of the repair-free house net profit, generated considerably more than the other two bonus schemes put together. Since Tier 1 payment was paid on actual profit produced, irrespective of whether it was growing or in decline, the incentive value of the other two bonus schemes, which were growth orientated, were severely undermined. Furthermore, since the bonus payments were made annually, there was little aspirational effect – the time gap between actual performance and receipt of the payment being too long.

The net result was that a payment system designed to stimulate growth and concentrate on improving pub profitability produced, at best, a neutral response from those it was designed to positively motivate.

A number of attempts were made to remedy the situation with some marginal improvements, but in 1987 the company decided to review radically its payment structure for pub managers. Two key objectives were defined: first, simplifying the current structure and, secondly, designing a reward system that focused managers' attention on growth and converting that growth in sales into profit.

Following detailed negotiations with managers and their union representatives, the existing system was dismantled and replaced with a new grading scheme and incentive bonus, the key components underpinning both schemes being growth and profitability.

Revising the grading structure

The grading scheme, which it will be recalled was assessed by reference to 14 factors, was replaced by a single component – the value of annual pub sales. A total of 32 grades were established, with take bands of approximately £300 up to grade 11 and approximately £600 at grade 12 and beyond.

The clear focus for pub managers was now that the single determinant for improving their grade and salary was to increase the takings in the pub – the growth factor. That incentive element was reinforced by having achievable steps in terms of the increased take required to move from one grade to the next.

In far too many schemes the amount of effort required to move from one grade to the next is disproportionate to the level of reward given, with the result that no one bothers or they attempt to manipulate the scheme.

The personnel purists will also be highly critical of the fact that there are 32 grades in the structure, being conditioned to the philosophy that the fewer grades you have, the more stable the structure is, the less complex the system is to administer. We need to confront that flawed philosophy: providing the scheme is soundly based, does it matter if you have 20 or 40 reward points? The more uniformity and constraint that is imposed, the more diluted the incentive value. If having more grades than convention dictates increases the administrative workload, and that is doubtful with computerized pay systems, then it's a price worth paying.

Changing the bonus scheme

The second area for review was the existing bonus schemes, these being replaced by a single scheme related to real year on year growth in pub profitability, with a payment to the manager of 20 per cent of net increase in profit. This meant a clear focus for pub managers on profit growth with a real, positive cash incentive for achievement.

A further important change has been in the frequency of payment. Applying the concept that the shorter the periods between the activities that generate reward and the payment being made, the more powerful the incentive value, bonus payments are now made at three monthly intervals.

Payment of the bonus to a manager is also an opportunity for the area manager to recognize the contribution made by the pub manager and, accordingly the bonus payment is made by individual cheque and handed personally by the area manager to the pub manager.

Monopolies and Mergers Commission – catalyst for change

The revised scheme for rewarding our pub managers continues to operate to this day in a large number of our directly-managed pubs and would have conceivably continued to operate in them all but for the advent of the Monopolies and Mergers Commission (MMC) investigation into the brewing industry during 1989.

Their report subsequently resulted in the MMC Tied Estate Order, one of its principal requirements being that companies that were engaged in brewing and operated 2000 or more retail outlets were required either to dispose of, or free from the brewery tie (a requirement to sell only brewery-produced or approved products), 50 per cent of the number of licensed premises in excess of the 2000 limitation.

The Allied Breweries group, of which Joshua Tetley is a regional trading company, had a number of options:

1. cease brewing;
2. reduce the number of pubs operated to below the 2000 limit;
3. comply with the MMC order.

Since Allied Breweries wished to remain in brewing and retailing, and operated some 6,730 licensed premises, it decided to comply with the MMC order. This enabled it to operate 4,365 licensed outlets under its direct control with 2,365 being offered as leasehold pubs or disposed of on the open market.

One of the consequences of this decision was the requirement to transfer a number of pubs from tenancy to a directly-managed pub system, the essential difference between the operation of the two systems being that managers are salaried employees, rewarded on the system described earlier, their freedom of action being fairly tightly controlled by company procedures and systems.

The tenant, in contrast, is self-employed, paying a rent based essentially on the predicted level of sales. Other than the restriction on selling company-produced or approved products, the tenant operated as a self-employed businessman or businesswoman. In simple terms, pub tenancies were probably the earliest form of franchise.

Over recent years the company had positively fostered the self-employed image and, as a small illustration, has retitled its first-line managers from tenancy area managers to business development managers. This change in title was far from being cosmetic in that, supported by a training and development programme, it represented a change in focus on the part of the business development managers from one of control to one of supporting the tenant in expanding his/her business.

Furthermore, the company, in transferring tenanted pubs to its directly-managed pub system wished now to retain a considerable number of its good tenanted operators.

Following a detailed review, it was concluded that despite the improvements made to the pub manager reward package, it was unlikely that this would be enthusiastically received by the tenants we wished to retain.

From cost control to business growth – starting the empowerment process

A further influence on our management thinking at that time was the desire to change the operating style and philosophy adopted by both the pub managers and their retail area managers. In a system heavily dependent on prescribed procedures and methods of operation, pub managers had, in most cases, limited opportunity to exercise any real decision making ability and, in turn, that led to the retail area managers concentrating on control issues such as bar staff wages and other cost issues.

In brief, we recognized the need to change our culture from one of emphasizing cost control to one of business growth; from one of hands on management to one where we could genuinely empower our pub managers. Empowering pub managers is not an easy process since they are, in essence, solus operators. One could almost describe them, in organizational terms, compared with their colleagues working at our main locations, as semi-detached managers. There is of course nothing unique about that, similar situations arise in the retailing of petroleum, newsagent chains, and a large proportion of high street retailing but it does require a further factor to be included in the empowerment process.

That further element arose from the fact that we wished to empower our semi-autonomous managers without losing control of the process. Therefore to the list of ingredients contained in the empowerment process eg, devolving responsibility, training and development, increasing employee knowledge and skill base, greater involvement in decision making etc, we can add the need to adopt a different approach to reward.

What was required was an approach to reward that enhances the empowerment process in that we focus pay and reward on those elements in the new relationship that we wish to foster and develop.

It was accordingly decided to review our payment system for the pub management group. While of necessity my comments will be restricted to this group at this stage, the rationale underlining our approach is capable of much wider application.

The review was carried out by the retail trade director and personnel director, the principle objective being to devise a payment system which would:

- provide more opportunities for individual pub managers to be both responsible and accountable for the day to day operation of their pubs.

- improve the level of financial incentive for pub managers;
- focus retail area managers on the key task of helping pub managers expand their business profitably;
- reduce central overhead costs by the introduction of a more devolved management style;
- increase the possibility of retaining tenants we wished to transfer to our directly managed pubs;
- positively assist in reducing labour turnover among existing pub managers.

In undertaking our desk research, it readily became apparent that only a handful of UK companies operated reward systems which came within the scope of the terms of reference we had set ourselves.

EMPOWERING MANAGERS – QUEENS MOAT HOUSES

One such company was Queens Moat Houses plc, a company owning a string of hotels in the UK and Europe. Of the group's 104 UK hotels two-thirds are operated through the incentive package and managed by what are known as Incentive Managers, the remainder operating through a conventional salary structure plus profit share.

The decision as to which scheme applies is based largely on the size of the hotel, the incentive scheme normally applying to hotels in the 50 to 100 bedroom range, and the degree of stability in terms of customer base.

For example, the Royal Moat House International, Nottingham or the Moat House International, Glasgow would normally be excluded from the incentive scheme since the managerial and financial responsibility would be considered too high for the individual operator.

Payment principles

The Incentive Manager package which attracted our interest is based on a number of simple but thought-provoking concepts, as follows:

- The manager is self-employed and is responsible for the employment, payment and motivation of staff.

- The manager is responsible for fixing pricing policy, menus, training programmes and so on.

- Queens Moat and the manager agree the amount of profit that the hotel will generate. The profit level for the hotel is based on anticipated turnover and an estimated profit return of from 25 per cent to 30 per cent for hotels with a large residential conference trade, to 15 per cent for hotels which are more dependent upon room and restaurant revenues.

- The manager is contractually required to return to Queens Moat the agreed profit return for each month. If revenues fall short, the manager has to make up the difference from his own resources and, equally, when profits exceed budget, as they normally do, he retains the whole of the surplus.

- The manager is responsible for planning the capital development of their hotels. When Queens Moat approve a proposal, the manager is required to repay the investment over a period of five to ten years depending upon the sum involved. The onus on deciding whether a development will pay for itself is very firmly on the individual Incentive Manager. Accordingly, it would not be too unfair to suggest that Queens Moat avoids the risk but ends up owning the asset.

- Giving the manager direct responsibility for the profit performance of his hotel enables the company to operate with an exceedingly lean corporate structure. The reporting relationship is simply from the hotel manager to one of two operation directors, with none of the considerable on-costs of the conventional hierarchical management structure.

What the papers say

The cornerstone of the system is obviously the equitable negotiation of the annual profit budget for each hotel. Set too high and managers are severely penalized. Set too low and the company does not get an adequate return on its investment.

In a report by Norman Pleshnell,[1] John Dedman, General Manager of the Moat House Hotel, Bournemouth, is quoted as saying 'I could not and would not consider working for any other group of owners' and quotes the incentive scheme as being the principal reason.

In his ten years at Bournemouth, John says that he has got the profit budget wrong on a couple of occasions, admitting that '1986 and 1987 were not vintage years as far as I am concerned, but they were very good years for Queens Moat Houses plc'.

He is, however, full of praise for the system and the way it operates. 'If you work like hell, you have the opportunity to make a very good living. The company will spend lavishly on refurbishments and improvements, although, of course, this will be reflected in an anticipated upturn in trade and profit levels. It works very well for me and very well for Queens Moat.'

So just how well does it work for the Queens Moat organization? Their financial report shows that turnover rose from £100.9m in 1986 to £484.5m in 1990. Pre-tax profits increased from £14.9m in 1986 to £94m in 1990, and net assets grew from £240m in 1986 to £1,169m in 1990, a profit performance a number of their competitors would love to emulate.

The Queens Moat incentive plan also requires an effective monitoring system in order that they can pinpoint any hotels showing signs of potential financial difficulties, the principle being to assist individual managers in overcoming problems rather than applying the 'dead hand' of bureaucratic control.

Commenting on the scheme John Bairstow, Chairman of Queens Moat, is quoted as saying:

It's an industry that runs on percentages; we know the averages for food and beverages; we have four-weekly reporting. If there is a major fraud it would show very quickly. We have only to see a 1 per cent drop and we very quickly ask the right questions, but we trust our managers and set up a bonus system for them. We have only had three leave since 1972.[2]

This latter point is of significance in an industry where high labour turnover is the norm. He continues by referring to the fact that hotel managers have to work long, unsociable hours but says 'providing there is reward, it will work'.

The Queens Moat model, with its accent on devolving responsibility to the unit operator supported by a highly focused reward system, was of interest to us and influenced Joshua Tetley's subsequent thinking on how to restructure the reward package for our pub managers. Obviously, simply to transplant the Queens Moat system into any other organisation could be a mistake, the key is to be selective and graft on those elements which will be absorbed and fit your own particular circumstances.

EMPOWERING MANAGERS AT JOSHUA TETLEY

It was from that background that the Joshua Tetley Retail Partnership Scheme was formulated by a working party consisting of members of retail management, personnel, accounts and marketing.

The principal focus of retail partnership is to encourage licensees to concentrate on the key business objective of increasing their pub turnover profitability within cost parameters. The key element is the reward package which is based on the weekly take of the pub. Against each of the take bands is an allowance to cover the costs of running the business. The cost allowance covers the manager's salary, staff wages, music and entertainment, cleaning materials, glassware and all the many other small-cost items associated with running a pub. The company remains responsible for the business rates, maintenance of the property, capital expenditure and marketing support.

The reward matrix is formulated as shown in Table 5.2.

Table 5.2 Reward matrix for the Joshua Tetley Retail Partnership Scheme

Take band	Weekly net take (VAT exclusive)	Cost allowance
	£	£
K	up to 2000	575
J	2000 – 2499	575 plus 9 % of wet take over 2000
I	2500 – 2999	620 plus 10 % of wet take over 2500
H	3000 – 3499	670 plus 11 % of wet take over 3000
G	3500 – 3999	725 plus 12 % of wet take over 3500
F	4000 – 4499	785 plus 13 % of wet take over 4000
E	4500 – 4999	850 plus 14 % of wet take over 4500
D	5000 – 5499	920 plus 15 % of wet take over 5000
C	5500 – 5999	995 plus 16 % of wet take over 5500
B	6000 – 6499	1075 plus 17 % of wet take over 6000
A	6500 or over	1160 plus 18 % of wet take over 6500

The twin focus for licensees is to increase the level of weekly take and accordingly move to a higher cost allowance band, and reduce the cost of running the business, the licensees being the net beneficiaries. The need for the scheme to be aspirational is met by the progressive percentages applied to the take bands and also by the payment being made weekly in arrears, the frequency of payment reinforcing the relationship between results and reward.

Since day to day cost control is now very firmly in the hands of the licensee, retail area managers can now concentrate on supporting them in developing and growing their business. This is achieved by both parties agreeing a business plan which is aimed at ensuring that budgeted take levels are achieved and that licensee income does not simply grow at the expense of pub standards and customer service.

Partnership on trial

A trial group of 20 pubs were selected, each of the licensees volunteering to take part. The trial commenced in September 1990 and continued until March 1991 and was undertaken to test the validity of the assumptions we had made, as well as ensuring that our administration systems were robust enough to cope with the Inland Revenue, VAT and internal requirements. In addition, and most importantly, we needed to gauge the reaction of both licensees and retail area managers to the acceptability of the scheme.

In the scheme review in March 1991, the licensees involved in the trial and their area managers and trade directors evidenced support and commitment for retail partnership to be formally implemented as an alternative to the current payment system. The results of the trial showed that, on average, licensees had earned £200 per week more than they would have received on the conventional salary package, this being due to a combination of increasing sales, better control on ancillary cost items and reduction in bar staff hours.

The last point is of significance in that the reduction in bar staff hours was not accomplished by reducing standards of service to the customer, but by the licensee and his/her partner spending more time serving behind the bar. Prior to the trial, licensees were responsible for around 13 per cent of all bar transactions, with a value of 10 per cent of total take. During the trial this increased to 21 per cent of all transactions with a value of 28.8 per cent of total take. While this change had an immediate effect on increasing the licensee's earnings it also has a medium-term effect on business growth.

Market research into the reasons why customers choose to visit a particular pub continually demonstrates that the presence of the licensee and the relationship he/she develops with the customer are prime ingredients in retaining and attracting those customers.

The trial also showed an increase in sales and controllable profit and the emphasis on building the business was reinforced by the introduction of a barrelage incentive scheme.

The final dimension was the reaction of the licensees and their area managers to the basic philosophy underlying the scheme. Both groups evidenced support, with licensees emphasizing the greater freedom and responsibility it gave them, and area managers welcoming the opportunity it gave them to concentrate on business development instead of day to day control issues.

A critical influence in achieving that position has been the amount of resources committed to the training and development of both the retail area managers and our retail partners to equip them with the skills required and, just as importantly, the self confidence to adopt their new roles with enthusiasm.

The results so far

The scheme now encompasses some 222 retail partners, 165 of whom were previously employed under the conventional pub manager salary package, and 57 ex-tenants.

Results as at August 1991 of the 35 pubs that had been trading for a continuous period of five months showed that, compared with the equivalent period last year, they had increased their total sales by 3.6 per cent and profit by 4 per cent. These results are particularly good when one compares them with houses not involved in the partnership scheme and with performance levels within the whole industry where, due to economic recession, a standstill situation in retailing activities is very much the norm.

The benefits of the scheme in performance terms are further reinforced by the data from the 15 pubs that have been conditioned to the scheme, including the trial period, for the ten months the scheme has been in operation. In those houses, compared with last year, total sales have increased by 9.1 per cent and profit by 8.1 per cent. All in all, a powerful reinforcement of the role reward can play in motivating employees; there is, after all, no superlative performance without a powerful reward system.

The impact of the Retail Partnership Scheme on our operations was recognised by *The Publican* magazine in their national award to Joshua Tetley as the 1992 'National Brewery Chain of the Year'.

HE'S HERE TO HOLD THE HORSES HEAD

The second example of securing major change through reward is within the company's distribution fleet.

In common with large sections of industry in Britain the brewing industry was no stranger to the major conflicts that occurred throughout the 1970s to the middle of 1980, the major area of vulnerability being the distribution of its products from the brewery gate to the pub.

That vulnerability is akin to that of the newspaper industry in that no one wants to buy yesterday's newspaper; equally, if you cannot get the pint of beer you want today you will either go to a competitor's pub or do without. You certainly won't buy two tomorrow to compensate for the brewery's failure to deliver today.

PBR in distribution

That basic weakness was exploited to the point of persecution by the distribution trade unions, reinforced by the payment by results (PBR) scheme they were paid under, aided and abetted by compliant management whose focus was on maintaining short-term profitability at the expense of long-term cost. The fact that history had taught us that paying Danegeld only results in our adversaries asking for more with increasing frequency was ignored.

A number of those symptoms were prevalent in Joshua Tetley during the late 1970s and early 1980s, the major problem being the operation of the distribution PBR system. Each activity that the driver and drayman undertook had a time value and the schedule was three pages long with time values expressed to four decimal places.

A constant feature of the scheme was the claims made by crews for compensatory payments for delays occurring inside the brewery and at customers' premises, increase or decrease in the size of containers delivered, difficulties experienced in delivering to particular pub cellars and so on.

From time to time management would rebut such claims with attempts to tighten up the work standards by reference to the improved roadway network, better handling facilities, improved vehicle design etc. The net result was that both parties were out of focus, their *raison d'etre* being the resolution of conflict rather than providing an excellent service to their customers.

This lack of emphasis on customer service was exacerbated by the operation of unrestricted 'job and finish' which meant that employees could clock off when they had finished the planned work allocation for the day. The difference between the planned and actual day worked was of the order of three to four hours per day, part of the difference being due to high effort working but due also to the slackness of the PBR standards. The net result was that the crew's focus was on completing the job in the least possible time, often at the expense of customer service.

As an illustration of how ingrained restrictive practises were in the brewing industry, one anecdote that circulated through the Courage group in the late 1970s related to an external consultant, hired by the company to investigate working methods. A crew of three men arrived in an eight-ton motor vehicle and were met at the pub by the consultant. After observing them unloading beer into the cellar for 15 minutes, he asked the driver and drayman what the third man was employed to do. 'Oh' they said, 'he's here to hold the horse's head!'.

In 1985, Joshua Tetley decided that it needed to undertake a fundamental review of its distribution payment systems, both to simplify the scheme and to improve the level of productivity. Following a series of negotiations with trade unions involved, it was finally agreed to replace the myriad of time allowances with two simple values – a payment for each barrel delivered and a payment for each mile travelled in delivering to the outlet. In addition, job and finish was limited.

Despite initial teething problems in crews coming to terms with the fact that every minor change would not result in an immediate revision to the barrels and miles payments, the scheme was successful in increasing productivity and significantly reducing conflict.

A new approach to reward in distribution

However, during the four years the scheme was in operation, a number of problems remained. The high gearing of the scheme and the direct correlation between reward and effort meant that crews continued to take short cuts which had a deteriorating effect on customer service. Safety standards were, on occasions, being jeopardized, and there was evidence of 'burn out' by crews in their late forties. Two further forces were also impacting on the company as we approached 1989. First, there was increased competition in the beer market, particularly in free trade, and retention of accounts in that area was particularly dependent upon providing a level of customer service superior to that offered by the competition. Secondly, there was a growth in the number of companies offering a contract distribution service at rates lower than those of our own in-house service.

The underlying reasons for the increase in organizations contracting out a whole range of services they would have previously operated themselves are described by Charles Handy[3] who maintains that increasingly organizations will resemble the shamrock, the three clover leaves representing the three different groups of people having some form of working relationship with it. The first leaf he describes as the core of qualified professionals, technicians and general managers who have jobs for life. The second leaf he suggests will comprise specialists to whom the organization will contract out all non-essential work. The third leaf will be made up of temporary and part-time wage earners hired to meet the peaks and troughs.

The twin thrust of increased market competition and economic forces resulted in our designing, negotiating and implementing a new reward scheme for distribution employees in September 1989. The scheme consisted of a fixed salary in return for delivering a fixed work load averaged over the year to recognize the peaks and troughs of the beer market. This had a direct impact on improving customer service, particularly during peak trading times.

Secondly, to meet economic considerations, the salary package paid significantly less for the same workload than the previous scheme, the effect on pay being mitigated by the application of an earnings protection scheme for a two-year period. In effect, it was anticipated that, over a period of two years, wage increases would basically bridge the gap between earnings generated by the scheme and previous average earnings. Thereby, the company achieved a two-year standstill in wage costs.

A small number of employees did not wish to participate in the salary scheme and they were offered, and accepted, the company's voluntary redundancy scheme. Rather than recruit new employees, the company decided to supplement its requirements by part-contract distribution since, even with the new pay levels, there was a cost advantage in so doing.

In the two years that the scheme has been in operation, the cost effectiveness of the department has improved. Customer service requirements are given a higher priority by delivery crews, the accident at work rate has reduced and we have a stable industrial relations situation.

The power of effective reward in achieving that and bringing about a changed attitude among employees cannot be minimized.

An alternative to overtime

Despite the reductions that have been achieved by employees in the length of the working week, and the investment that has been made in technology throughout British industry, overtime working continues unabated. In fact, during the period 1981 to 1991 overtime working in manufacturing actually increased from 8.5 hours to 9.3 hours per week.[4]

A major issue for most companies, particularly those employing large numbers of blue collar employees, is the control of overtime.

Prior to September 1991, non-staff employees in Joshua Tetley were paid by reference to an hourly rate based on the grade of job, with hours being worked in addition to the standard week receiving a premium ranging from time and a half to double time. Due to a period of investment in new plant and teething problems associated with major changes in technology, employees had become conditioned to a high overtime site. While cooperation between employees and their managers and supervisors, and improved operational standards, had made considerable inroads into previous high levels, they remained in excess of the budget for the year.

As will be recalled from earlier comments, the danger with basic rate payments that are supplemented by overtime premiums is that earnings can, and do, fluctuate in accordance with individuals' pay needs rather than production requirements. Despite the control systems that management can implement, I would suggest that below a certain level we can only control up to 10 per cent of the actual overtime hours worked – the tip of the iceberg. This was the stage we had almost reached by September 1991.

We were also cognizant of the fact that we were quickly approaching the situation in which, once we reached our budgeted overtime levels, any considerable reduction below that level would reduce our competitiveness in the labour market with the attendant problems of retention and recruitment.

On the other side of the coin was the fact that reducing overtime below the budgeted levels would represent a major cost saving to the company in reduced energy and associated costs and enable us to provide an even better service to our customers. A not unfamiliar conundrum for management.

In reviewing the options available, we discarded a number

of alternatives including productivity bargaining, our experience reflecting that of a number of organizations in that paying for the removal of one set of restrictive practices merely results, in the medium term, in a further list being created. We also wished to 'free up' individuals in terms of what they and their team could contribute rather than applying the common denominator of collective bargaining.

As a consequence of those self-imposed parameters, the following scheme was designed, the details of the scheme being briefed to employees as follows:

HOURLY PAID EMPLOYEES – OVERTIME REDUCTION SCHEME

1. *Introduction*
   This scheme has been developed in support of the company's objectives of:

   1.1 achieving production requirements as far as practicable within normal hours.
   1.2 achieving efficiency.
   1.3 reducing costs.
   1.4 improving customer service
   1.5 rewarding employees for co-operating with any changes necessary to achieve the above objectives.

2. *Scope*
   The scheme will apply to all Leeds based, hourly paid inside workers (ie, it excludes those distribution employees who are conditioned to a salary based payment system).

3. *Effective Date*
   The scheme will be effective from Period 7 (1991/92) and its operation reviewed at the financial year end (March 1992).

4. *Scheme Detail*

   4.1 The scheme is designed to encourage employees to support measures that will minimize the need for overtime working without jeopardizing production requirements and to reward them accordingly.
   4.2 An overtime budget for each of the employee groupings below has been set for the current financial year (1991/92). These budgets include the cost of all overtime (including 21st shifts) together with the cost of premium pay for working normal hours on a statutory holiday.
   – brewing process
   – packaging

- container refurbishment
- warehouses
- stables
- Benyon park
- engineering

Budgeted overtime levels may be subject to immediate review as a consequent of any major fluctuations in trade.

4.3 Employees who are required to work overtime hours (or normal hours on a statutory holiday) will be paid the appropriate premium rates at the time in accordance with current agreements.

4.4 If the total cost of such overtime/premium pay hours is less than the budgeted figure, the 90 per cent of the difference will be shared equally amongst employees participating in the scheme *pro rata* to their attendance (ie, excluding overtime).

4.5 The formula to determine the money available for distribution to employees will be:-

Number of hours (below budget) × average hourly rate × 1.6 × 90 per cent.

4.6 Payments under the scheme will be made quarterly as soon as practicable after periods 3, 6, 9 and 13. Payments being subject to normal deductions.

4.7 The cost of any overtime or normal hours on a statutory holiday required but not worked (excluding sickness) will be deducted if production requirements have been jeopardized in any way.

4.8 New starters/leavers who are in the company's employment on the payment date will receive a pro-rata payment.

5. *Methods of achieving overtime reductions*

5.1 Details of overtime/premium hours paid will be published each period to enable employees to see hours actual performance is comparing to budget.

5.2 Departmental managers will hold regular meetings with employees/ representatives to discuss ways in which overtime working can be minimized.

Early indications are that the scheme has been welcomed by managers and employees alike, with constructive debates regularly taking place on how it can be more effective, how we can work smarter. A significant change from the previous attitude of 'how can we generate more overtime?' or 'plant breakdowns are management's responsibility'.

REWARDING THE TOP TEAM

Finally we shall comment on the reward system for the board and executive management. Their salary range is determined by the grade for a particular post, with salary increases and progression being determined by the performance review system, the performance rating being assessed against quantifiable key objectives. In addition, a bonus scheme applies based on total company profit performance for board members, and a combination of departmental and company performance for executive managers.

The reason for the distinction is interesting in that highly geared bonus schemes, as well as increasing the level of individual and departmental competitiveness can, as a by-product, introduce an element of divisiveness with common goals being sacrificed for departmental self interest. As a consequence the scheme deliberately focuses on departmental and company performance for executive managers and on the sole element of total company profit for board members. To ensure that the scheme contains some aspirational element, payment is made half yearly.

The principal reason for outlining the changes we have made to our reward systems since the mid 1980s is to illustrate that the philosophy outlined in the early parts of this section are capable of being applied and implemented in a highly unionized environment.

Visible rewards

Earlier we made the comment that there are no superlative performances without a powerful reward system. That comment is true both within companies and in life in general. In childhood our achievements are so often the product of parents or grandparents setting the right expectations for us, and reinforcing that achievement by some form of appropriate reward. Consider the reward and recognition that comes from being the best in a particular sporting activity. One only has to observe the faces of athletes as they mount the podium to receive their Olympic gold medal to appreciate that thrill and the deep satisfaction they experience from being acknowledged as the best. For each of them that piece of metal is ample reward for all the self-sacrifice and long hours of dedicated training; ample reward in that the occasion is one of the most visible events in the world. In designing reward and incentive schemes account needs to be taken of not only the visibility of the event but equally the visibility of the reward itself.

Since few if any managers share what they earn in salary and bonus with their neighbours the visibility factor has to be reserved for the non-cash and fringe benefit area. It is however an area that has tremendous potential for motivating employees in general and talent in particular.

The company car

Of all the fringe benefits the company car has no equal in terms of its visibility and its capability to telegraph to foe and friend alike an individuals position in the corporate hierarchy. It's a matter of fact that the type of company car sitting in your driveway probably says more about your level of income than you would ever admit to neighbours or acquaintances.

Over the last 30 years the growth in the number of company cars has been phenomenal, generated during regimes of high personal taxation by the relative advantage of lower taxation rates being applied to benefits in kind. While the benefit deriving from the company car increasingly attracts the attention of the politicians, its possession is still highly regarded within the ranks of management. Highly regarded not simply because of its financial benefits – economics does not rule all our behaviour – but more because of its perceived value and the visibility of our status it provides within the organization. Some indication of its perceived value is provided by consultants Buck Paterson Ltd: in a recent survey of readers of their magazine 87 per cent of males and 83 per cent of females rated the benefit of a company car and free fuel highly.

As the number of job holders entitled to a company car has grown, so to has the complexity of most companies' car policies. Long gone is the situation I experienced at Cadbury's in the late 1960s when a colleague and I were the first two managerial staff to have a company car and, with the exception of a policy on the provision of bicycles to plantation foreman in the Gold Coast, no company policy existed on the subject. Today in most companies the company car policy is the bureaucrat's delight, with the minutia of the type of trim, number of wing mirrors, type of radio and so on, taking up page after page. The downside is that a benefit designed to motivate can, badly administered, create frustration and demotivation. Within sensible limits car policies need to be more flexible. Is their any logic in the family man being able to obtain an estate car, while the young or post-menopausal executive is denied access to high performance models? Most car policies believe so.

A further point that is not without its sense of irony is the situation within a number of companies who, in pursuit of equal status policies, have dismantled status-based dining facilities, abolished clocking, introduced common sickness and pension schemes but continue to operate the most obvious form of status, the company car. I do not make any value judgements one way or the other. I only highlight the inconsistency, an inconsistency that will be all too apparent on the shop floor.

Vouchers

So far most of the employee incentive programmes I have referred to have been cash based, however it would be erroneous to assume that cash based schemes are the only form of efficient incentive. In fact a growing number of companies are introducing incentive schemes based on a mix of cash and non-cash reward.

Increasingly the non-cash element is taken in the form of vouchers which, in terms of the goods and services they can be exchanged for, are virtually as flexible as cash. The UK's first ever voucher was probably the all too familiar book token, now over half a century old. It was during the 1970s that vouchers began to be used in sales incentive schemes, and during the last ten years or so their use has expanded both in terms of the number of vouchers on the market and the number of employees coming within the scope of such schemes. In fact it is estimated that there are well over 200 different vouchers in use in the UK in a growing market currently valued at over £300 million per annum.[5]

The attraction of basing part of an incentive programme on non-cash rewards such as vouchers is that, unlike cash bonuses which get lost in the salary cheque or absorbed into day to day living expenses, vouchers have to be spent separately on something tangible. It therefore follows that the luxury items that were purchased or the snaps of the holiday chosen are a permanent reminder of the performance that gave rise to the award and, equally, an indication to friends and relatives of the regard in which the company holds the recipient. A further factor in their popularity is that vouchers are currently National Insurance Contribution and VAT free and as such, offer savings to both employees and employers.

A further variation of the voucher system is the 'Green Shield' type of glossy brochure which illustrates a range of goods and services available, each one having a points value. Each of the company's incentive programmes has a points value which can be exchanged for goods in the catalogue. The advantage for the individual is that he can either cash in his points immediately for a smaller prize or save them up for a major gift.

One of the benefits of the catalogue system is that the scheme is capable of being shared with the family, who will encourage the individual to perform at work at a higher level. The use of the family in intensifying the incentive effect is described by Brian Friedman as 'the nagging spouse factor'.[6]

Incentivising training

Whilst most voucher incentive schemes generate reward when specified targets on, for example, sales, quality or cost are met, the concept is increasingly being applied to training. The principal exponents of this approach are de Brus Marketing Services Ltd who, working with a number of major high street retailers, have developed a comprehensive system for tracking the effectiveness of staff training in a range of activities from product knowledge and customer service, to selling techniques. At the end of each training module employees complete a questionnaire, the form being mailed to de Brus who evaluate the answers. The individual receives points for the number of correct answers which are exchangeable for goods from the gift catalogue. In addition to the motivational effect on individuals, the data captured enables companies to independently assess the quality of its training and equally in large organizations, particularly those with high labour turnover, provides an accurate measure of the coverage of its training.

The above are all examples of how a little creativity can add to our reward packages. Perhaps from time to time we need to supplement the activities of our remuneration experts with a representative or two from the marketing department.

SUMMARY

In this chapter we have concluded that:

- The five principles of reward can be applied throughout the organization, leading management to adopt a focus and perspective different from that dictated by conventional wisdom, across most, if not all, employee groups.

- Reward is a key influence in determining behaviour at work, and telegraphs to everyone in the organization those actions it values.

- While the empowerment process has traditionally concentrated on devolving responsibility, training and development, greater freedom in decision making and so on, the retail partnership programme demonstrates that reward has an equal part to play in that process.

- Organizations need to appreciate fully the power of visible rewards in motivating employees in general, and talent in particular. We equally need to exorcise bureaucracy and the functionaries from the remuneration department and replace them with creativity and innovation.

REFERENCES

1 Pleshnell, N (1988), *Food and Drink Magazine*, May.
2 Kay, W (1988), *Money Observer*, July.
3 Handy, C (1989) *The Age of Unreason*, Business Books, London.
4 *Employment Gazette* (1992) Historical Supplement no 3, June.
5 Buck Paterson Consultants Ltd, *Viewpoint*, Issue no 16, April 1992.
6 Friedman, B (1990) *Effective Staff Incentives*, Kogan Page, London.

Fish Don't Applaud

At the start of this section I used two key works – reward and recognition – both being essential tools in the continued motivation of talent. Use one without the other and we will never capture the full potential that our employees bring to their jobs every working day. Equally we have to set the right expectations for our subordinates, they have to be stretching but attainable. We have to provide the right degree of reward and recognition. Inappropriate reward and recognition can be as demotivating as no reward at all. So now let us turn to the area of recognition.

MEMORABLE MANAGERS

All of us, at some time or other (and let's hope that for you it's been the majority of occasions), have worked for memorable managers. We've also worked for the reverse.

One of the key elements that separates the two is the ability of the memorable manager, spontaneously and naturally, to recognize exceptional performance. Several leading figures have been kind enough to share their experience of working with memorable managers with me.

Firstly, Professor David Weir, Director of the University of Bradford Management Centre. David warmly recalls the experience of working for Sir Monty Finniston, formerly the Chairman of the British Steel Corporation, who had the capacity for 'thanking you hard when you did a good job and equally kicking you hard when the reverse occurred, in both cases you knew what message you were supposed to get'. David, who is today an accomplished platform speaker, recalls an occasion in his early days of attempting to be humorous about engineers in an after dinner speech to the Council of Engineering Institutions. After the speech Monty Finniston came up to him and said 'Don't make speeches in public again'. As David Weir recalls 'that criticism was harsh, but I took the message, got my material in order and learnt how to do it right'. Subsequently

Monty Finniston invited him to join him in speaking on a number of public platforms and as David Weir says he was always unstinting in his praise for a well delivered paper, and always prepared to take time out to share one or two thoughts on how to be even better.

For Gordon Elliot his early career showed little promise of the entrepreneurial flair he was later to demonstrate. Leaving school at 15 years of age a succession of manual jobs led him to working for Kleenezee, the door to door selling organization. It was at that time he worked with Ron Brake, an Area Sales Manager. For Gordon that was a momentous period in his life, for the first time he met someone who recognized that he had a natural talent for selling. Not only that but Ron Brake was able to instil in Gordon the tremendous enthusiasm he had for selling and a belief in the product he sold. As Gordon describes: 'Ron Brake not only developed the talent I had, but more importantly, he helped me to believe in my own ability'.

Recognizing that his lack of academic qualifications and broad understanding of business would be a limiting factor in his career, in 1979 he commenced part-time studies at Leeds Polytechnic. Some five years later he graduated with a BA (Hons) degree, and today is Managing Director of Defenco Security Services Ltd, with 290 employees and a turnover of £2 million. As Gordon says, 'my career is a testament to Ron Brake; he saw in me what others failed to recognize'.

In a career that has taken him from the schoolroom to the House of Commons and finally to the House of Lords, Viscount Tonypandy's talent and respect for his fellow men has been recognized not just by parliamentarians, but by the world at large. It was, however, as Speaker of the House of Commons that he is probably best known to the general public, with the broadcasting of Parliament providing a national audience for the mellifluous tones, the wit and wisdom of Mr Speaker Thomas.

While George Thomas undoubtedly inherited the Welsh love of words and language and had a natural talent for public speaking, this ability was influenced and stimulated by the local miners' leader in his home town of Tonypandy. George describes how, in his early years:

> my friends and I visited his home to study the art of public speaking, his unfailing emphasis was on:
> 'Prepare thoroughly and know all the facts concerning your argument.
> Be courteous to those with whom you disagree.

Humility: do not presume that you know everything, because you don't.
Watch your appearance: the first impression people have of you is what they see'.

This influence has remained with him throughout his life.

Armed with a law degree, a master's degree in organizational theory and a career that has exposed him to the rarefied atmosphere of corporate life at Unilever, Tony Lochery would be the first to admit that, at the age of 29, he still viewed the business world from the standpoint of the theorist. At that time, he says, 'my perception of the way a company made profit was through a text book. Right or wrong was a function of logic and strategy was everything'.

That is, until he met Tom Farmer, the chairman and chief executive of Kwik-Fit. Having left school to start work as stores boy at a tyre company and today chairman of a multi-million pound organization, Tom Farmer enjoys folk hero status in the Edinburgh business world. While on the surface Farmer appears to rate opportunism as highly as strategy, his critics are ever watchful of his entrepreneurial skills.

With that backcloth, it's hardly surprising that when Tony and Tom met it was a meeting of opposites. However, Tom was sufficiently impressed by Tony to offer him the job as director of strategy for the Kwik-Fit group. Offered, as Tony recalls, with the accompanying illumination from Tom Farmer that 'short-term strategy is what we will do this morning; medium-term strategy is what we will do this afternoon; and long-term strategy is what we will do tonight'.

Looking back over his career, Tony Lochery readily says that working for Tom Farmer was one of the most exciting and challenging periods of his business life. From those experiences he cites, in particular, appreciating that, above all, successful management is as much about personal leadership as it is about strategic direction. It's this latter point about personal leadership with Tom Farmer as a role model that has probably had the most impact on Tony's career.

Three years on, Tony runs a dynamic and rapidly expanding training and consultancy company with a turnover of £3 million. It's perhaps a tribute to both men that Kwik-Fit is that company's largest customer.

For Rhiannon Chapman, among a series of firsts that have dotted her career to date, being the first personnel director of the Stock Exchange and the first female director of the Industrial Society in its 74-year history, are particularly noteworthy. Among all the individuals she has both worked with and for, the legendary George Mepham was to have an effect that has impacted on her approach to management to this day. As she says, he was one of life's natural delegators in that 'having established the range of my activities, he left it to me to decide how to go about my job, but at the same time however, he made it clear that he enjoyed hearing my ideas and talking them through with me. In particular he did not shy away from telling me when I had gone wrong, which was at least as important as his generous acknowledgements when I did something well'.

However, it is when Rhiannon describes George Mepham's reaction to a 'once in a lifetime promotion opportunity' that came her way that we begin to understand the impact he had on a succession of subordinates. When Rhiannon told George she was on the short-list for a senior personnel post in a major factory in the group, he told her that while he had hoped she would stay with him longer, he would do everything to help her application.

Just before she went for the interview, he called her into his office to tell her about some plans he had for developing her current job further and asked her views on them. Rhiannon insists that he was clearly trying to limit the damage for her should she not succeed in the interview – she did.

Rhiannon Chapman's experience vividly illustrates that the effective development of subordinates owes little to the bureaucratic systems that appear to drive most company development systems, but in reality, suffocate them. Nor does it owe a great deal to supply-driven and expensive external training programmes.

The reality is that effective subordinate development is dependent on selecting managers who naturally and spontaneously delegate, reward and recognize and coach members of their team to the next level of performance – the George Mephams of the world.

Finally, from my own experience of working for a number of memorable managers, the one that had the most impact was Ken Marriott, formerly Group Personnel Manager for Cadbury-Schweppes. For him, everyone in the organization was a person of significance, irrespective of job title, and this he demonstrated by his total concentration on what you wished to discuss with him, irrespective of the myriad of problems he had to face that day. I often try to mirror Ken's amazing patience when I am discussing with someone a question that to them is of the utmost importance, but to me is not significant compared with the rest of the day's agenda. I don't always succeed but it doesn't stop me trying.

Equally Ken was one of life's natural developers of people. One quickly appreciated that he was always driving and guiding you to conquer new horizons, and gained as much satisfaction from your achievements as you did yourself. Furthermore he always ensured that your achievements were recognized throughout the organization.

THE POWER OF RECOGNITION

That the power of recognition in stimulating and maintaining high performance should be so little understood and used by the majority of managers is a tragedy. Not just for them, in that they never realise the full potential of their subordinates, but equally for their companies in the lost opportunities for individuals to make a more significant contribution to the wealth of the organization.

But the real losers are the subordinates themselves as they are denied the inspirational effects of having their talents recognized and experiencing the real job satisfaction of being encouraged to move up to the next level of performance.

The question that should hang on every manager's office wall is:

If you perform at a level of excellence and nobody recognizes it, why should you repeat it tomorrow?.

The means of recognition are many and varied. They range from simple recognition of a job well done, by the use of a simple thank you – a well-worn phrase but effective if sincerely meant – to the more formal means of recognition through major awards and gifts. A universal law is that:

We tend to do well what others applaud us for doing.

A neat illustration of that is a story relating to Bob Hope, the entertainer. On his 80th birthday he was interviewed by a television presenter who asked him: 'now you've achieved your 80th birthday and been listed in the ranks of the top 50 richest men in the States, why don't you retire and go fishing?'. Bob Hope paused and replied: 'I've considered it, but fish don't applaud'. We tend to do well what others applaud us for doing.

That philosophy is now well ingrained into the management culture of Joshua Tetley, with reward and recognition for high performers having a high priority.

NEW WAYS TO SAY THANK YOU

Most of us during our day to day activities will thank members of our staff for doing a job really well and, on occasions, will write to individuals formally thanking them. The impact of such messages can be considerably enhanced by resisting the temptation of dictating them into type and taking the time and effort to hand write them. People enjoy receiving such recognition, but can we do more?

I suspect that most of us, when we have received such letters, either consign them to the bottom drawer of our desk or place them in our 'insurance file' to await the day when our performance might be called into question and they can be produced in self-defence.

One positive way of reinforcing personal thank you messages has been conceived by SRI, and is known as 'drops for your bucket'. It's based on the simple philosophy that the uncaring manager believes that in life we are all born with a bucket of self-esteem and for that manager the more praise he ladles out to individuals the lower the level of self-esteem in his bucket. For that type of individual the only way he sees of raising the level is to get his ladle into your bucket, this he or she will do when they take all the credit for a job you have done well.

The caring manager, in contrast, knows that the more credit or praise he ladles out to subordinates the more he defeats the law of basic physics – the level in his bucket rises to overflowing. As Dr Clifton of SRI says,

> the unyielding secret of the bucket and ladle is that when you fill another's bucket it does not take anything out of your own bucket. The level of your own bucket gets higher when we fill another's and, on the other hand, when we dip into another's bucket we do not in reality fill our own . . . we lose a little.

Messages of praise and thank you are written on the card illustrated in Figure 6.1 overleaf.

A further derivation of this type of personal acknowledgement is the five star award used by Talent + (Figure 6.2 on page 121).

The stimulating effect on the individual receiving the five star award is further reinforced by the back of the envelope being overprinted as shown in Figure 6.3 on page 122.

Figure 6.1 A new way to say thank you

This approach can be adapted to ensure that it is appropriate to individual company circumstances. In my own industry, Simon Milne introduced the 'Bottles for your Cellar' card, to acknowledge the contribution of high performing licensees (see Figure 6.4 on page 123).

Figure 6.2 The Talent + five star award

What is interesting is that no one has been told what to do with them but almost everyone who receives one notices the hole in the top of the card and pins it up on the office wall. A far cry from the letter we consigned to the 'insurance file'.

IF YOU FRAME IT, WE HANG IT

We equally apply the same principle when we receive certificates at the end of training courses. Most of us have received certificates, diplomas, etc, during our college and working life and where do we consign them? In most cases its to the bottom of the sideboard drawer.

In Joshua Tetley every certificate we award is framed by the company before it's handed to the recipient, the simple reason being

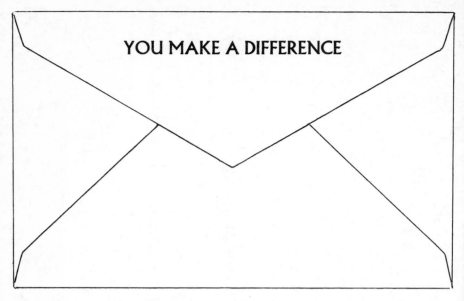

Figure 6.3   Talent + five star envelope

that *if it's framed we hang it*, and, in so doing, are visually reminded daily of the success we achieved.

Recognition, in addition to endorsing an individual's contribution, can also be a means of stimulating competition. A number of such schemes operate within the company:

- Member of Bar Staff of the Month;
- Licensee of the Month;
- Pub In Bloom Competition;
- Best Christmas Decorations;
- Cellar of the Year Award;
- Master of Ale Award.

All are positive ways in which Joshua Tetley recognize high performance and stimulate competition.

For the individual, the prize he or she receives, the plaque that hangs on the wall of the pub, the publicity in the house magazine and, on occasions in the local press, are all an endorsement of the effort they have made and a mark of the company's appreciation.

Within our tenancy and retail departments the most prestigious event is the annual gala dinner when the retail director, tenancy

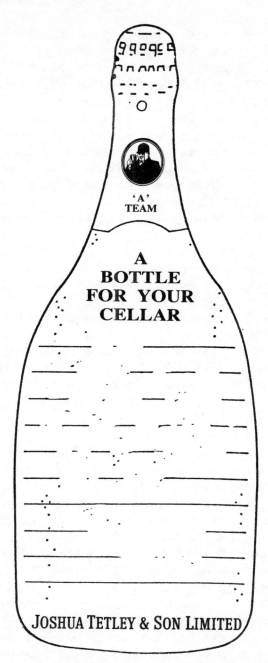

Figure 6.4   The Joshua Tetley thank you

director and their trade directors invite their top performing licensees and their partners. Being invited to this Top Performers Dinner is again a reinforcement of the company's appreciation of their efforts and provides an appreciative audience for the winners of the top awards. In addition, it stimulates competition – it is not unknown at these events, as the top couple go up for their major award, for a wife to clutch her husband's arm and say 'We're going to be up there next year'.

In our free trade sales department, like most selling operations, promotional events for customers and sales staff are very much the norm. Pride of place, however, is reserved for the Salesman of the Year award and the Sales Manager of the Year award. Points are awarded for performance against key targets and the results published in the monthly Canvas Brief. Since, by nature, salesmen are competitive, the monthly results are keenly awaited to see who is at the top, and so on.

Both the Salesman and the Sales Manager of the Year awards are made at the annual free trade sales conference, normally by the managing director. The awards have varied from holidays on the QEII to a video-camcorder for Mick Jones who has won the Sales Manager of the Year award for the last three years. One year he had his company car upgraded to an Audi 90. Discreet enquiries in the department revealed that this was the car Mick had always wanted to drive. Giving individuals some degree of choice in the award they receive, or finding out their preferences, is important.

Appropriate rewards

It may seem an obvious point, but we all have varying needs and interests. Nevertheless in some organizations this fact is ignored with the same type of award being made year after year.

Doug Rath, president of Talent +, illustrates the importance of the appropriateness of awards in a story of the salesman who, on receiving a plaque the previous year for being the most outstanding salesman, made it clear to the company president that he hated plaques. The next year he was again the company's top salesman and, when the company president called him up to receive the award, he refused to go up and accept it. The president was furious and felt he had been humiliated in front of his 500 salesmen and their wives. He turned to Doug and said 'I'm going to fire him'. Doug replied, 'Firing your top salesman is like indulging in self-flagellation'. Instead, Doug's reaction was to look for an alternative reward.

Knowing the salesman had no interest in plaques, they needed to find out what did motivate him. In talking to the salesman Doug discovered that what he was really proud of was his wife and two daughters. As the following year's event came close, it was clear that the same salesman was going to receive the top award again. Doug obtained a photograph of the wife and two daughters and commissioned an artist to paint a portrait from the copy.

At the awards dinner that year everyone knew that the same individual was once again the top salesman of the year. The question in the room was not who had won it, but would he go up and receive it? Announcing the winner the president said that the award this year would be a little different. As he called the salesman up, the president unveiled the portrait of his family. Tears ran down the salesman's face as he received the painting. He later confided in Doug that 'it was the proudest moment of my life'.

So let's take that lesson on board and make sure our awards are appropriate. Equally, we need to ensure that the form that the competition takes is applicable to individual needs and performances. While most of the examples I have used have related to peer group competition we need to be appreciative of the fact that not everyone is motivated by this type of event and that our incentive programme must be flexible enough to accommodate people motivated, for example, by individualized goals and targets.

KEEP RE-HIRING THE BEST

While recognition for sales staff is fairly commonplace, on the shop floor it is rare. That this is so is more a reflection of our lack of imagination than of our employees' ability to respond to such schemes.

Within Joshua Tetley, reward and recognition schemes apply across the company. In our brewing process, packaging and warehouse departments schemes operate for hourly paid employees and are based on achieving key targets of quality, service and efficiency. Results are published monthly as is the amount of cash generated for that month. Actual payment is made three monthly, with team members deciding what form the reward should take. It is not unknown for a department to buy equipment for their favourite charity, rather than sharing the cash across the group.

Rewarding and recognizing employees for achievement against key targets underlines their importance to the business and focuses employees' attention on those targets. Managers are also encouraged to give spontaneously small gifts in recognition of a job well done, or for excellent service provided.

The return to the company from giving a bottle of champagne or wine to a licensee or member of bar staff for a particularly outstanding event, or providing free beer tokens to a production shift that has worked extremely well, far exceeds the small cost involved.

When Martin and Bernie Tremlett became the first couple managing a Joshua Tetley pub to achieve wet sales of over £1 million in a year, the occasion was marked by a formal presentation by the company's retail director at which they received a luxury VIP trip to Royal Ascot on the legendary Orient Express. This trip fulfilled a lifetime ambition for Bernie.

Company newspapers and house magazines are also an ideal vehicle for recognizing our top performers. Well written copy and quality photographs are appreciated by the recipients as well as providing role models for the rest of us. In a world where talent, by its very definition, will always be in short supply we need, as Jack Falvey, the American management author says, 'to go out from time to time and re-hire our best performers'. By which, of course, he means that we, as managers, need to give them the time, attention and emotional support we gave them on their first day.

Taylor Walker travelling pullman style

Setting the right expectations for employees and reinforcing their achievements through reward and recognition programmes are valuable ways of retaining our best performers. Equally they provide a ready means of putting the spotlight on the role models we want other employees to emulate.

One company that fully appreciates the impact that reward and recognition can have in creating an aspirational environment within the company is Taylor Walker. David Longbottom their Managing Director describes how on joining the company he noticed on the wall of the company dining room six photographs of managers who had achieved annual profits of £100,000 or more. A keen advocate of rewarding achievement David decided to embrace the concept into his company plan and enhance the reward element. Subsequently it was announced that every manager who achieved annual profits of £100,000 or more would be invited with his partner to a VIP day, travelling champagne-style in a private pullman train. In addition, every area manager with a qualifying manager would be invited to help host the occasion.

In the first year the number of qualifying participants had grown from 6 to 30, and last year a total of 250 participants, including hosts, took part. Recognizing that to be effective incentive schemes have to be aspirational Taylor Walker have introduced a 200K Club and a 300K Club. Membership is conferred on those managers who achieve annual profits of £200,000 or £300,000 respectively with members and their partners being invited to a prestigious day out, the choice of destination reflecting the distinction in achievement. Each of the participants receives a gift and a certificate commemorating their membership of the Club. In 1990 12 managers and their partners attended the 200K Club event and 5 managers and partners the 300K Club. In reviewing the results for 1992 David is confident that he will see an increase in the number of managers breaking through the £200,000 and £300,000 barriers.

One further interesting fact is that four out of the five top profit earners in Taylor Walker had periods of service between 7 and 17 years. It is, I am sure, not too presumptive to suggest that the reward and recognition scheme introduced by Taylor Walker rekindled their talents and will equally ensure that they remain with the company for the long run.

One is sometimes asked if we can give too much recognition. Let me respond by asking whether any one of you reading this book has received so much recognition from your boss or your company over the last month that you couldn't accept just one more thank you. The answer, of course, is no.

No negative recognition

Finally let me conclude by emphasizing that in the talent led company the concept of negative recognition does not exist. The whole emphasis is on catching people doing things right, not the reverse. This is in marked contrast to an experience I had at the Sheraton Hotel, Newport Beach, California when, on admiring the glass fronted trophy cabinet of awards for the co-worker of the month, employee of the year and so on, I spotted on the bottom shelf the award for the bitch of the year. The lady in question had won the trophy for two consecutive years!

Or the conference I was recently speaking at when at dinner at the end of the day's session, the managing director or the company concerned announced to the audience of 150 managers and their partners a new award for the 'Wally of the Year'. He proceeded to list a number of administrative infringements the individual had committed, then announced his name, called him up to the front of the audience and presented him with a four foot high toy monkey. From the chill that went around the audience it was obvious that it was only the managing director who thought it was amusing. Later that night when I spoke to the individual concerned he told me it was the most humiliating experience of his life. Spoof awards in your own peer group can, in the right situation, be amusing, among superiors or subordinates it can be denigrating.

The second component in our talent equation then is to positively reward and recognize our high performing employees. Properly used it is the high octane fuel for stimulating people into action, achieving goals they never before thought attainable.

SUMMARY

In this chapter we have concluded that:

- The continued motivation of talent relies as much on the formal and informal recognition the organization extends as it does on its official reward system. The degree of recognition must accord with the performance achieved since inappropriate recognition can be as demotivating as no acknowledgement at all.

- The means of recognition range from the sincere 'thank you' to high profile presentations at company functions and are all, in their own way, effective in reaffirming the behaviour the company values as well as introducing a degree of healthy competition.

- In many organizations the problem is not that they are unable to apply their collective imagination to recognition, as evidenced by the product promotion drives that frequently operate for the sales force. It is rather an inability to appreciate that such schemes can be effectively extended to everyone.

THE FIVE ISSUES FOR THE BOARD AGENDA

1. Ensure that we are positively rewarding employees – we should do more than just pay wages and salaries.

2. Define the behaviour we require from employees to achieve our company objectives and ensure our reward systems reinforce their achievement.

3. Create reward systems that enable our employees to influence directly the measures upon which they are being rewarded.

4. Ensure that the level and frequency of payments emanating from bonus or incentives schemes are aspirational.

5. Provide opportunities for publicly applauding and recognizing our best performers.

► PART 3 ◄

What Managers Really Want and How We Can Give it to Them

7

Creating the Vision

In this third section we want to examine in greater detail those ingredients that combine to create an organization that is able to effectively respond to individual and group expectations from work, expectations that are in accord with and supportive of organizational goals. The challenge we will be exploring is how we can make the key motivators of a shared vision, responsibility, achievement, self-fulfillment and personal growth become more widespread, enhancing talent as people progress through the company. As part of that process we will examine ways in which we can improve our level of investment in higher quality training, development and career management.

As will be discussed further, a prime requirement for organizations is to provide a compelling vision of the future. That vision should provide a focus for all our day to day activities and assist us in putting into perspective the organization's aims and objectives.

In the talent led organization the mission or vision statement, has a further important purpose; that of providing a framework within which talent can coexist with the achievement of both individual and organizational goals. As will be appreciated talented people are often demanding and are not normally compliant, but you cannot expect such individuals to be a lion in the field and a lamb in the office. Anyone who doubts the power of an effective mission in welding talent into a potent team should be reminded of the Live Aid concert. There, a number highly individualistic, talented pop stars came together as a group, sublimating their individual differences and rivalries in pursuit of a greater good.

The reality, however, for a large number of those we employ is that diffidence and low expectations are the norm. Sir John Harvey-Jones, commenting on managing out of the recession,[1] says that managers:

> will need to guide their staff through the process of continuously adapting and improving which will be essential to cope with the forthcoming decade of change. A key part of this task will be

to encourage people to shrug off their natural diffidence and lack of ambition by broadening their perspective of what they are capable of achieving.

The suggestion that a large number of our employees display diffidence and lack of ambition may come as a surprise to those of us who are fuelled by job satisfaction and ambition. That this is the reality for a large number of our employees, and in some cases those that manage them, was suggested by Dr Anthony Daniels in an article published in the *Daily Telegraph*,[2] in which he maintains that a large proportion of those being treated in hospital or seeking medical advice 'have no physical illness' and, in reality, are suffering from having unsatisfactory lives. As a consequence, he claims, large numbers 'suffer from boredom and from a vague but powerful resentment that gnaws insatiably at their heart'. He continues that such individuals have little or no interest 'indeed, many of them have no conception of what it is to be interested in something or any idea of what concentration is. These people do not even understand my question'.

From interests he moves on to ambition, illustrating that few have any real ambitions. He concludes by saying that 'the most one can say is that daydreams are, to them, what ambitions are to Americans'.

While most of us would conclude that this is a somewhat over-dramatised account, it does contain, at the very least, a suggestion of the truth of the lives of many of those we employ. That this should be either wholly or in part a representation of the situation is no denigration of the individuals themselves, more a reflection on society today and on how we manage people at work. As Herzberg reported,[3] the majority of employees' needs include advancement, responsibility and achievement. That a number should display total disinterest in experiencing those three commodities of industrial life says more about our ability to manage effectively than it does about them.

We need to correct that situation since one of the key ingredients of our success model is the ability of an organization's leaders to harness the abilities of everyone in the organization and to view employees as an asset in which we consciously and consistently invest.

DESIGNING THE MISSION STATEMENT

The first step in the process of harnessing that often untapped individual potential is to create the vision.

In a study by Korn/Ferry International and the Columbia University Graduate School of Business[4] most of the respondents agreed that one of the key requirements of chief executive officers was to 'convey a compelling vision of the corporation's future'. The vision, the mission statement, provides a powerful sense of focus and direction for everyone in the organization, as well as enabling us to relate easily to the organization's goals.

All of us in an organization, irrespective of status, need the stimulus of a worthwhile purpose to the job we do to help motivate us into action. That vision, that mission statement, must be aspirational. That oft-quoted mission that President Kennedy gave to NASA in 1960: 'We will put a man on the moon by the end of the decade' is a prime example.

From industry, Federal Express's 'Absolutely, Positively and Overnight'; Nissan UK's 'We aim to build profitably the highest quality car sold in Europe'; or restaurant chain Golden Corrall's 'To make pleasurable dining affordable' are equally powerful. However, my personal favourite of all the one-liners is the undoubted apocryphal story that suggests that the unofficial mission of Fuji Film is 'Kill Kodak'.

In designing, or perhaps reformulating, the company's mission statement, it's necessary to bear in mind three golden rules:

1. It should be capable of being summarised in one line.
2. The goal should be within sight but just out of reach.
3. You should be able to recall it ten minutes after you first heard it.

The more words you use the more you dilute its impact. As Barry Hopson and Mike Scally[5] say 'people will march for a sentence but never for a paragraph'.

That lesson is lost on a large number of companies who continue to produce mission statements by the yard and then wonder why their impact is diluted and fails to become part of the everyday vocabulary of employees.

Further examples of mission statements that fail to work come from companies which communicate via the 'bill stickers' approach to life. They produce their mission statement in poster form, deluge the shop floor and office walls with the message, then stand back to see what happens. The result is often little or nothing. Employees have grown too sophisticated to be influenced by such crude devices, very often describing them as propaganda.

LIVING THE MISSION

One common feature of highly successful companies is that they are headed up by chief executives who are visionaries and are able to share that mission, that purpose, with everyone in the organization. While they recognize that written communications through bulletins and company magazines, and briefing through line management, have their part to play, they equally understand that they are no substitute for the top team walking the job. Popularised by management theorists as MBWA (management by walking about) it presents an unparallelled opportunity for making face to face contact with employees, not simply to listen to employees' views but to reinforce the company's mission.

For Tom Farmer, chairman of Kwik Fit, it provides the opportunity for reinforcing his creed that 'retailing is selling things that don't come back, to people who do'.

For Michael Eisner, president of the Walt Disney Corporation, it provides the moment to share with employees the mission of their founder Walt Disney 'do what you do so well that people who see it will want to come again and tell a friend'.

In a world driven by bottom line profit considerations, endless meetings and conferences, the sight of the chief executive or his top team walking the job is an all too rare event. Yet it wasn't always so. A large number of directors and managers of the Victorian and Edwardian era, unfettered by the latest fashion in management thinking as prescribed by the business school or the most popular management guru, spent time most days 'at the coal face'. For them, like Tom Farmer, or Michael Eisner, it was an opportunity to show employees that there was a human face to top management; to see what was really happening on the shop floor rather than relying on reports from subordinates; to reinforce their mission by talking face to face to employees.

In addition to all those advantages, regularly walking the job is a positive reminder to all employees that their job is so important that you are prepared, in spite of all the other day to day pressures, to set time aside to meet them and share some of their day to day problems.

Management by working about

But why stop there? Management today not only needs to be visible it also needs to be seen as credible in the eyes of employees. The reality in most companies is that executives and senior managers have lost touch with the basic tasks people perform at work. The days of managers proudly claiming that there was no job on the shop floor they couldn't do is long gone in most companies. In retailing just ask senior management to operate the till system and you will, more than likely, receive the answer that 'I know how it operates in principle'. What employees on the shop floor need to know is that you know how it works in practice, and thereby have confidence that in making strategic decisions you will be aware of the impact on day to day operations.

We need to import into our management vocabulary the concept of *Management by Working About*, by which we mean managers should not only possess the basic craft skills that the product or service is based on, but on an annual basis demonstrate that they are still able to perform them effectively. While most managers will initially feel threatened by such a proposal, in Golden Corrall it's a well established practice, where most managers enjoy demonstrating that they can operate at a level of competency equal to their best operators.

The reinforcement in Joshua Tetley for directors to walk the job and visit our pubs is the strap line 'there are no tills in the Tetley boardroom'. But all is not lost. A recent survey by Smythe Dorward Lambert,[6] the communications consultants, found that 'two-thirds of British companies have started culture change programmes to improve employee performance'. From the list of techniques that companies said they would use to manage the change, 62 per cent felt that 'a mission statement outlining the organization's goals and objectives helped staff understand how their job fitted in and helped motivate them'.

For some organizations the mission statement is such a cornerstone of the organization's philosophy that prospective employees who cannot relate to, or accept the organization's mission are rejected for employment. One such organization is Cancer Treatment Centres of America. Their mission statement is: 'The pursuit of the cure of cancer'. Any prospective employee who does not believe that cancer can be cured is not employed.

In view of the importance placed by them on the belief factor, it's perhaps no coincidence that in a recent survey of patients, in answer to the question 'Why did you choose Cancer Treatment Centres of America?' the most common response was 'They build better relationships with patients – they treat the whole person, not the disease'.

HOW EFFECTIVE IS YOUR MISSION STATEMENT?

Having a well constructed mission statement is, however, only step one in the process of influencing employees' attitudes and perceptions. The second, and more difficult task, is ensuring that all our executive and managerial decisions are in accord with the principles underlying the statement itself. If they are not, then widespread disillusionment and cynicism is the natural outcome, producing behaviour totally at odds with our original intentions.

To be successful, mission statements have to be seen as the filter, the gauze of our decision making model and, if our decisions are rejected by the fine mesh of the mission statement as being incompatible, then we do not proceed.

One acid test of the effectiveness of the mission statement is to ask employees what they get paid to do. If there is no reference to the customer in the answer, we are back to the drawing board. One superb example of an individual who was able to conceptualize the company's mission statement was the barman at the Bulls Head, one of the Joshua Tetley pubs. One morning when visiting the pub I saw him picking up litter from the car park which had blown from the adjacent fish and chip shop. I asked him what he was doing and he replied 'I'm selling pints of bitter to customers'. In that answer he demonstrated that he understood that the outside of the pub as well as the inside had to be clean and inviting to customers.

Moreover, in a world where the talent we require will always be in short supply, we need to communicate our vision to the outside world. This will involve us in changing the thrust of PR and marketing activities from a wholly product driven strategy to one aimed equally at selling the company as an employer. Companies with a clear vision and business philosophy that marks them out from the competition will have a head start, particularly those with values and philosophies that prospective candidates wish to be associated with. In short, we have to become the company in our market sector that individuals want on their CV. In the late 1960s this was typified by Mars – job applicants often said that two years with them was as good as five years with any other employer.

Getting the company's vision and philosophy across to the public will involve all senior management in the organization, not just the specialists. In particular, company chairmen will have to adopt a much higher profile. Gone is the time when they could be dismissive of the small group of their peers who capture the headlines of the business and financial press. They will have to be as expert at selling their company as an employer as they are at selling the company's financial performance to the city.

In the talent led company the mission, the vision statement, has a particularly important role in not just simply focusing our activities, but providing the framework within which talent can exist and co-exist with the pursuit of the organization's goals. Management equally have to accept that their day to day activities and actions will be measured by employees in as much as they are, or are not, in accord with the company's mission.

SUMMARY

In this chapter we concluded that:

- The company mission statement should provide the vision – the focus – which enables employees to direct their activities. In the talent led organisation it has one further important function – that of providing the framework within which talent can exist and co-exist with the pursuit of a shared goal.

- The mission statement must be inspirational as well as aspirational. Of the 'three golden rules' of mission statement design perhaps the most vital is that you should be able to recall it ten minutes after you first heard it.

- Chief executives and senior management need to live the mission, adopting a higher profile where the action really takes place, be it on the factory floor, the office complex or the high street. Management, however, needs to do more than practice management by walking about; it equally needs to practice management by working about.

- Living the mission also requires organisations to ensure that their decisions fully reflect the sentiments contained in the mission statement. If they do not, and the reality is pious statements surrounded by poor quality decisions and actions, then cynicism is the natural outcome.

REFERENCES

1 Harvey-Jones, Sir John (1991) 'Managing Out Of The Recession', MSL International Boardroom Briefings, August.

2 Daniels, A (1991) 'How Can We Minister To The Real British Disease', *Daily Telegraph*, 5 June.
3 Herzberg, F, Mausner, B and Synderman, B (1959) *The Motivation To Work*, John Wiley, New York.
4 'The 21st Century Report' (1989) Korn/Ferry.
5 Hopson, B and Scally, M (1991) *12 Steps To Success Through Service*, Mercury Books, Gold Arrow Publications, London.
6 Smythe, Dorward, Lambert (1991) *Personnel Today*, August.

8

The Management Malady

Organizations that are desirous of recruiting and retaining talent will have to possess the ability to see corporate life as it is in reality, rather than how they would perceive it, and have promotional and development policies that match that reality. Perhaps one of the best sources of the fiction of organizational life is the company recruitment brochure where careers are regularly described as a smooth continuous development, with each promotion being a stepping stone, towards a visible destination. The reality, in contrast, is one of managerial turbulence with careers being enhanced and retarded by the increasing phenomenon of company takeovers, mergers, acquisitions, technological change and economic factors. A reality where, for most managers, change is the constant and stability is the exception.

THE THREE YEAR MANAGER

Evidence to support this view has been provided by Nigel Nicholson and Michael West in their research on the career development of 2,000 middle to top level managers and executives in the UK.[1]

The fact that change is the constant in industrial and business life was demonstrated by over 33 per cent of managers reporting that the single, most important 'life event' that had occurred over the previous 15 months had been a 'significant business reorganization or major organizational change'.

The fact that job change is a frequent event for managers was evidenced by the steepening decline in the number of managers in the UK who spend their entire working lives with a single employer, from one-third of all managers in 1950 to less than one in ten today. Two-thirds were with their fourth employer compared with less than 25 per cent in the 1950s and 1960s.

Further evidence of the rate of management volatility is provided by the fact that three years was the average duration of job tenure, with one in ten having had five or more jobs in the previous five years.

In a number of organizations, a three year average might not be considered a rapid mobility rate and this would be so if the job changes were merely incremental moves up the organizational ladder within the individual's basic discipline or profession. However, Nicholson and West bring together a formidable array of statistical data to suggest that over half of management job changes involve both a simultaneous change in status ie, promotion and a change in function. Of that group, around 50 per cent achieve both promotion and a radical job change by moving out from their present companies to new employers.

The reasons for increasing job mobility among British managers are equally revealing. Of the 17 responses elicited by Nicholson and West as to the reasons for the last job change, the top six were:

1. To do something more challenging and fulfilling.
2. As a step towards career objectives.
3. To change career direction.
4. To improve my standard of living.
5. To acquire new skills.
6. I saw no future for me in my job.

Since increased material benefits ranked fourth, any image of managers chasing from job to job in sole pursuit of a bigger salary cheque, plusher company car, or fatter perks, is severely dented. The simple reality is one of seeking more challenge and self-fulfilment from work. The tragedy for companies is that almost three times as many managers had to leave their present employers to find that challenge as found it through internal promotion.

These indications of disenchantment with conventional careers by experienced, mature executives have been described by a number of commentators as an illustration of a reduction in the work ethic by society at large. 'Not so', says Robert Goffee, Associate Professor at the London Business School. He maintains that the current attitudes displayed by both young and older managers do not mean less commitment to work itself, more 'a seed corn change in commitment to a different form and a preparedness to seek out other forms of organization in which to channel their energies and talents'.

Goffee believes that a number of reasons can be attributed to this change in attitude citing, in particular, the large scale reorganization, down-sizing and cost-cutting programmes that began in the 1980s. While this may have resulted in organizations being leaner and fitter it 'had a dramatic and traumatic effect on managers'. In particular, flatter organizations meant more plateaued careers and fewer promotional opportunities.

During this period there was a lack of attention by companies to the survivors. Their sympathy was expended on those who left – often buttressed by five-, and in some cases, six-figure pay-offs. For those who lived beyond the restructuring, being asked to do more with less became the norm. A consequence of this was 'an increase in working time, reduced ability to take holidays and a rise in stress related illness'.

DISILLUSIONMENT IN THE MANAGEMENT RANKS

The manifestations of a growing disillusionment with a lifetime commitment to corporate life are many; the fact that it applies indiscriminately was brought home to me in 1989. I was speaking at a conference in Oxford organized for young managers aged between 25 and 30 years, a large number of whom had either completed or were about to complete an MBA and were judged by their sponsoring companies to be 'high fliers'.

In answer to the question 'what are your long term career goals?', 55 per cent were desirous of exiting from organizational life to run their own business, 25 per cent were aiming to retire by the age of 50 to pursue their leisure interest full time and were able to demonstrate a degree of financial planning that could make it achievable, with only the remaining 20 per cent wishing to pursue a lifetime corporate career.

While it is easy to be dismissive of the aspirations of the young, it is abundantly clear that, for the majority, their long-term ambition is to avoid a lifetime commitment to corporate life. This situation is certainly in stark contrast to that of 20 years or so ago when similar groups, with few exceptions, would have demonstrated a convincing commitment to a long-term managerial career.

Interim management

But is this dissatisfaction with managerial life just a malaise of the young? Evidence to suggest that it is not is confirmed by the number of seasoned executives and managers offering themselves as candidates for interim management.

In addition, as Godfrey Golzen[2] points out, interim management is emerging as part of a new pattern of career options with people remaining in salaried employment for only part of their working lives. Targeting on a market of seasoned executives aged 45 years plus, interim management has emerged over recent years as a powerful alternative to conventional recruitment and resourcing practices.

Interim managers offer their management skills and experience to companies on assignments lasting normally between three and nine months. They distinguish themselves from conventional consultancy in that they are directly responsible to the board of the company to which they are assigned and carry full executive authority. Typical assignments range from business turnaround, preparing a subsidiary for sale or integration of an acquisition, to bridging the gap following an unexpected departure with no clear successor identified.

That executives are seeing this area of employment as an alternative to the conventional career is demonstrated by the growth in the number offering themselves as candidates. In the five years since interim management became established in the UK, John Hird, managing director of Albermarle Interim Management Services Ltd, has received over 10,000 applications from individuals who wish to join their interim register – and the trend is growing.

Joining the ranks of the 20 or so companies offering this service is the PA Consultancy Group. Despite the fact that they did not publicly announce the establishment of an executive leasing division until early January 1991, by November 1990 Martin Wood, their director, had received over 800 applications from aspiring candidates.

Since the success rate of those wishing to join interim management is as low as one in ten, the ranks of British management must contain a lot of frustrated individuals. They are somewhat reminiscent of the POW's of the last war – always turning up for the morning and evening roll call but spending their productive time trying to tunnel out of the company compound.

Promotion

Is it not equally conceivable that part of that frustration, and often reported management disenchantment with a long-term commitment to corporate life, is more a reflection of how organizations' promotional policies operate than any real absence of drive and ambition within the ranks of British management.

Evidence to suggest that this is so is provided by a series of attitude surveys conducted by PA Management Consultants among managers and executives within Joshua Tetley. In a series of questions that related to individual perception and attitude to promotion one question asked 'In terms of your career development, do you see your present job as:

A. the peak of your career?
B. a stepping stone to further promotion?
C. a bit too demanding?

The results of the survey on this question were as follows:

36 per cent answered A;
62 per cent answered B;
 2 per cent answered C.

Of the group surveyed, 80 per cent were aged under 50 years and 20 per cent were over 50 years. In refining the data to those in the age range of 25 to 40 years, the number seeing their present job as 'a stepping stone to further promotion' increased to 75 per cent. In the 'highly talented' group it rose to 96 per cent.

It therefore follows that our promotional policies need to ensure that our most talented individuals are identified at an early stage as having potential and are developed accordingly. The benefits of doing so are twofold: first, by providing high talent with the opportunity of experiencing the stimulation and satisfaction that derive from advancement and greater responsibility, we enhance the possibility of their retention within the business. Second, we enhance the economic performance of the organization since we have already established that talent makes a greater contribution to productivity and profitability.

The question we therefore need to raise is whether our current promotional policies and employee development programmes support the attainment of those objectives? From a review of 50 company policies and programmes on these two subjects it appears clear that most focus on job performance, attainment of prescribed academic qualifications, acquisition of leadership skills and career planning, with exposure to and experience of key functions as the route map to the executive dining room. Unfortunately this admirable list of attributes only explains why some individuals achieve pre-eminence in their organization and others, who appear equally promising, do not.

The reality is that throughout the UK tomorrow's company bulletin announcing yet another round of reorganization, restructuring, reshuffling of the pack and consequential promotions and demotions, will be greeted with a range of mixed emotions through-out the organization. The list of ennobled subjects will be a source of avid speculation as the reader attempts to unravel why some made it and others, equally talented, remain in the second XI. It's an all consuming topic of conjecture, whether the conversation is held in the senior common room or the works canteen.

For those at the threshold or mid-point of their career, the reason why candidate A and not B succeeds is a constant source of speculation and consternation as each attempts to find the answer, in the hope that it will provide the solution for themselves. For the highly talented the topic is all consuming as they search for clear evidence of merit and equity in the decision. But the answer is as elusive as the quest for the philosopher's stone. Certainly most universities and management schools provide little in the way of guidance to aspiring students.

Those company promotional policies that have been published tend to be of the exhortative school, with the central message that if you keep your eye on the ball, your shoulder to the wheel, your ear to the ground, you will be successful – which conjures up the picture of today's successful manager as being a somewhat 'athletic Quasimodo'.

HOW TO GET PROMOTED

Well, if we are going to understand better the key attributes that lead to success, what better place to start than to discuss the question with those that have reached the number one spot in their organization. From a base that already takes for granted the components of ability, intelligence and work ethic they would distil the following key features as being the ingredients that lead to get-ting in the fast track and moving through the management hierarchy.

John Holmes, chairman and chief executive of Holmes & Marchant, who in 20 years has built his organization to 22 companies, with a turnover of £60 million, says that the key to success is to distinguish yourself from the rest of the pack:

Individuals will not succeed unless top management know of their existence, their desires and ambitions. People who do not get noticed get overlooked and left behind. It's about having charisma, style and flair.

For Matthew Bullock who was appointed, at the relatively early age of 40, as regional director of Barclays, Yorkshire and Humberside operations, the key is innovation – the ability to deal imaginatively with both today's and tomorrow's potential problems. 'Discover the 10 to 15 per cent of changes you can introduce successfully rather than dissipate your energies by adopting a machine gun approach to every problem in the organization'. To that he would add, 'the need to understand your own strengths and weaknesses and build a team around you that reflects the areas in which you need support'.

From a perspective that combines experience both on the field and off the field in the boardroom, Peter Gilman, chairman of GMI Construction and vice-chairman of Leeds United Football Club says 'Good managers in industry, like successful club managers in football, have the innate ability to select talent and to build a winning team around them'. He continues, 'successful managers plan meticulously, they leave nothing to risk, spend time investing in their people and inject some glitz and fun into the atmosphere'.

From the profession that spends it's whole time identifying fast track performers, former head-hunter Bill Fitzhugh says that successful executives display a high level of self-reliance. 'There's no reluctance to being exposed to risk taking and being responsible for decision making. They take a high profile in the organization and are not the courtiers of life'. In particular, they have 'the ability to handle conflict positively and the interpersonal skills to continue to build positive relationships with those they disagree with'.

For Sir Michael Craig-Cooper of Carre Orban & Partners, early career decisions are of paramount importance in terms of the profession entered and the company chosen. 'Job seekers should enter a profession that is going to enable them to gain the widest business experience and exposure and join companies that are the leaders in that market sector'. Having highly regarded companies on your curriculum vitae can often make the difference between being short-listed and not. He also suggests that successful executives have taken 'the responsibility for managing their own career, and taken time out from the day to day to ensure they are managing it effectively'.

On the other side of the track, Ron Hopkins, regional director of the outplacement organization Drake Beam Morin Ltd, says that 'one common feature of displaced executives is their inability to react sufficiently to changing company culture and market conditions'. In particular he emphasizes that individuals have to understand that, on average, their immediate boss will change every three years bringing with him or her a different management style and list of priorities.

Successful managers are flexible enough to deal with those changes and have the interpersonal skills necessary to establish very quickly good working relationships with the new incumbent.

While all of those comments contain some useful indicators as to the reasons why certain individuals get to the top and their equally talented colleagues do not, do they provide a total answer? Based on day to day experience of organizational life one has to conclude that at least one piece is still missing from the promotion jigsaw.

HOW TO REALLY GET PROMOTED

Evidence to support that conclusion is provided by Fred Luthens, Professor of Management at Nebraska University who discounts most of the traditional management literature, classical theories and prescription as to what are the key ingredients that affect an individual's promotability.[3]

The classical school of management recommends such elements as the ability to plan, organize, staff, direct, co-ordinate, report and budget as being the determinants of success. On the basis of having studied over 400 managers during a four-year period, Luthens first explodes the discrepancy between commonly held beliefs and expectations about what managers should be doing, what the academics think they are doing and what they actually do. In practice, he found that managers devoted the major proportion of their work activity into four key areas:

- *Routine communications* – exchanging information; handling paperwork.

- *Traditional management* – planning; decision making; controlling.

- *Networking* – interacting with outsiders ranging from active involvement with public relations activities to customer/client relations; socialising and politicising.

- *Human resource management* – motivating/reinforcing; disciplining; managing conflict; staffing; training and development.

Second, he poses the vital question of whether there is any difference in the amount of time devoted to these four key activities by those managers who are described by organizations as *effective* compared with those judged to be *successful*?

Effective managers were defined by reference to unit effectiveness in terms of both quantity and quality of performance, subordinate satisfaction and subordinate commitment to the organization. Successful managers were identified by reference to promotional velocity – the speed at which they advanced, and the level they reached in the organization.

The question of definition – and there is clearly a difference between the two groups – is important because most people who have worked in organizations suspect that, from time to time, those managers who produce results and have satisfied, committed subordinates are not necessarily the ones who get promoted relatively quickly. Luthens' research shows that those managers who were defined as effective spent their time on the four core management activities as follows:

Routine communication	45%
Human resource management	27%
Traditional management activities	15%
Networking	12%

In contrast, those managers judged successful by reference to speed of promotion spent their time differently:

Networking	48%
Routine communication	28%
Traditional management activities	13%
Human resource management	11%

The findings of the success and effectiveness analysis would appear to support the view that networking activities are a way of getting ahead in the organization but have little to do with the contribution to effectiveness. They would certainly support the notion that those who experience rapid promotion are good at, and pay a lot of attention to, social and political skills. On the other hand, effective managers give more attention to communication and human resource issues.

As Luthens says, these conclusions have significant implications for today's organizations. Not least, how we can align our formal reward systems to enhancing those activities which increase company effectiveness rather than individual promotability.

While Luthens' research confirms the phrase most of us learnt at our mother's knee – 'It's not what you know, it's who you know that counts' – it also has a far deeper significance. It is just conceivable that the fact that there is a difference between successful and effective managers may help to explain the cause of some of the problems being faced by a number of major organizations? Furthermore it is conceivable that part of the growing disillusionment among management ranks is due to the realization that those who are effective in terms of their unit's performance and the management of its people are not necessarily the ones in the organization's fast track for promotion?

As a recent editorial column in the MSL International 'Boardroom Briefing' points out: 'The rash of fallen idols amongst the top management stars of the 1980s is eloquent witness to the difficulty of identifying the enduring qualities which characterize a successful director'.[4]

Grasping the promotion nettle

The fact that a good senior manager does not necessarily make an effective director is widely understood in most organizations and is not the problem. The problem is that they do not systematically practice it.

The result is that good managers are over-promoted and consequently are often eventually asked to exit from the organization. The loss of a once-effective manager and the resultant aftermath of human misery for the individual concerned is one we need to consciously avoid.

Compared to the way in which most organizations systematically evaluate investment decisions, and so on, the strategic appointment of directors and key executives comes a poor second best. We, therefore, need to import into our promotion policies and practices the same degree of objective evaluation. We also need to be honest with individuals as to how we see their future careers progressing in the organization. On their present performance do we see them as promotable or not? Managers and executives who are assertive on so many other matters often duck this fundamental issue.

While being forthright with individuals on this question may result in some leaving the organization, is it not preferable to their soldiering on in the mistaken belief that promotion is just around the corner? The net result being that the organization reaps their disillusionment when they inevitably come to the realization that further promotion will not come their way and they have left it too late to be marketable to other companies.

The reality is that, in that situation, *as many managers retire into their current jobs as leave through normal retirement,* spreading their discontent and cynicism among all they come into contact with.

SUMMARY

From the above analysis we can summarize the six basic problems facing organizations as follows:

- Widespread dissatisfaction with a lack of promotional opportunities and the consequential plateauing of careers.

- Lack of opportunity for individuals to develop their career from the specialist functions to a generalist role.

- Managers wishing to exit from their current organizations to find a more challenging and fulfilling role.

- Other forms of employment eg, interim management, new business ventures, being viewed as more attractive than conventional careers.

- Dissatisfaction with current management development systems and the level of training provided.

- Insufficient regard to the real cost of high management turnover.

Before we turn to the question of what steps organizations need to take to resolve these fundamental issues we need to turn our attention to the current training debate. In particular we need to expose the myth that simply committing more resources to training and development will in itself act as an instant remedy for all our problems.

REFERENCES

1 Nicholson, N and West, M (1988) *Managerial Job Change: Men and Women in Transition*, Cambridge University Press.
2 Golzen, G (1992) *Interim Management*, Kogan Page, London.
3 Luthens, Hodgetts and Rosenkratz (1988) *Real Managers*, Ballinger, Cambridge, Mass, USA.
4 MSL, August 1991, 'International Boardroom Briefing'.

9

Don't Teach the Pig to Sing

In the current training debate British management stands accused of not spending enough on training and developing its workforce. The prosecution, armed with surveys and research studies funded by government agencies, the TUC and private sector consultants, argues that Britain's performance at home and abroad is being handicapped by a lack of training.

TRAINING – THE POLITICIANS' PALLIATIVE

The argument attracts many adherents, ranging from government ministers and opposition spokesmen, to trade union leaders and training specialists. It seems that hardly a day goes by without the government announcing yet another new training initiative, and the opposition unveiling a new set of alternative proposals. The basic problem for both groups is that there is a degree of confusion as to whether their principal aim is to improve training radically, reduce unemployment or, at worst, provide a means of simply massaging the unemployment statistics.

The degree to which training has become politicized can be illustrated, from among a number of statements made by politicians, by a quote from opposition spokesman, John Prescott, that the sinking of the Greek cruise liner, *Achille Lauro* in 1991 'showed nobody spent enough money on training for air-sea rescue'.

Labour spokesman on economic affairs, Lord Preston, also entered the fray with a comment that 'The principle of leaving training to employers has failed'. But do we in management deserve to be castigated in this way?

A recent report, 'Training in Britain', by the government's Training Agency reveals that the total training effort is 'considerable', with 1.5 million man-years undertaken in 1986–87. This was the equivalent of 7 per cent of total man-years worked and the cost was around £33 billion. Employers played a significant role in funding that investment, sponsoring around 660,000 man-years of training at a cost of £18 billion. Conservative estimates would suggest that, with the acceleration of employer-funded training in the past three years, the figure today is above £22 billion.

Where concern will rightly be expressed is over the fact that a fifth of all employers do not provide any training. Furthermore, training in Britain tends to be concentrated among younger people with a good education. The chief beneficiaries tend to be the few, about 12 per cent, who have a qualification above A-level standard.

However, the belief that lack of training is the chief barrier to economic growth is simplistic in the extreme. Of equal importance are low capital investment, inefficient working practices and poor industrial relations. The argument that we can spend our way up the international league table by simply committing larger resources to training is not well-founded.

A NEW PHILOSOPHY FOR TRAINING

For far too long management in the UK has approached management development and training from the standpoint that, given sufficient time and resources, anyone can be trained to do anything. Large numbers of training specialists approach training from the viewpoint of the Jesuits: 'Give me the boy until he is seven years old and I'll give you the man'. In other words, if we have a problem in the organization, let's mount a major training programme has been the philosophy.

Sometimes training can be the solution, but it shouldn't be a Pavlovian reflex to every problem the organization encounters. The net result can be that *we attempt to train people to be what they are not*.

Perhaps the inherent weakness in that whole philosophy is best exemplified by Golden Corrall, the American restaurant chain. Ted Fowler the company's president has a sign on his office wall as shown overleaf.

Of course, from time to time we have to engage in remedial training but it should not be the central thrust of our training and development activities. In far too many organizations, training is seen as organizational first-aid, the sole means by which we correct or remedy individual deficiencies. The inadequacy of the philosophy is exposed when we ask ourselves how training can transform an individual with low courage into a highly assertive one. At best, training will merely provide a few techniques to mask the problem.

Never try to teach a pig to sing –
it wastes your time and annoys the pig.

It will not convert him or her into a person with the easy confidence to accept challenges. Equally, training will not convert a manager who is a low developer of staff into a high developer.

At it's best, training in management development will assist managers in understanding the theory – the way the system works. It will do nothing to remedy the root symptom of the low developer: an inability to derive satisfaction from seeing a subordinate grow and progress through the organization. The insecurity experienced by this type of manager when faced with talent will continue to manifest itself, no matter how much training he or she has on the subject.

In organizations where we are seeking to put success back on the boardroom agenda, we need to implant a new philosophy for training and development, one that accepts and appreciates that *training refines and develops talent – it does not create it.*

The essential point that has escaped most organizations is that *management can build on strengths and develop talents but cannot create them where they do not already exist.* Yet throughout the UK vast training resources are being committed to correct weaknesses rather than building on the strengths that individuals have.

Pursuing a talent led training philosophy can have a considerable impact on company performance.

It will be recalled that in Part 1 I outlined that over a five-year period Joshua Tetley had been tracking the performance of its 25 most talented public house managers compared with that of 25 managers with low talent. The top talented group increased its profit by 166 per cent; the low talent group by 55 per cent. The significant point to add at this stage is that both groups had been exposed to the same amount of training. In essence the problem with far too many companies is that they *try to raise the standards at the top by training the bottom*. These results support that view.

TRAINING FOR PROFIT

The new philosophy says too that if training and development are to enjoy a large share of company resources, measuring the impact on profitability, quality and service must become the norm, not the exception. Equally, education and training must be seen as something we invest in rather than consume, and we must measure the return on that investment.

But as the Training Agency report demonstrated, only 19 per cent of employers had made any attempt to analyse the benefits of training and fewer than three per cent had undertaken any cost benefit analysis. While exhortations from the great and the good will have some effect on the amount of resources companies commit to training, the greatest stimulus will be that they see a real return on their investment.

A common weakness throughout the personnel function in general and the training department in particular is the reluctance to measure regularly the impact of their activities on the key performance indices the company values. It is almost as if we have talked ourselves into the mental stupor that cost/benefit analyses, contribution to profit, and so on, are the sole prerogative of the finance function.

As Oscar Wilde said in a totally different context: 'All women become like their mothers. That is their tragedy. No man does. That is his'.

In the same way, bequeathing the analysis of the contribution of the personnel/human resources function to the cost centred approach of the accountants is a tragedy for the company in general and the personnel function in particular. The personnel function needs to measure more accurately and consistently its contribution to bottom line profit and in doing so will ensure that it obtains sufficient resources to maximize the benefits that people can make to the organization's growth. We therefore need to ensure that the training and development of our managers reflects this and equips them to be competent in undertaking the multi-functional skills they desire, and the organization will require, as a consequence of becoming a competitor, not just in national and European markets, but also increasingly in global markets. As companies embark on such strategies, new demands will be placed on those in the organization. A key feature will be their ability to handle the new circumstances positively and productively.

As Arthur Miller, founder of People Management Inc, succinctly put it: 'Maybe giants can dance – but can you know who amongst your managers will be moving to the beat and who will be trampled underfoot'.

Selecting talented managers and training and developing them to their strengths will ensure that we will all move to the beat of success.

SUMMARY

In this chapter we have concluded that:

- The over-emphasis by government and the majority of employers' associations on the quantity of training provided is misguided. A more important and fundamental question is the quality of training and whether we are getting an adequate return from our investment.

- We need to implant in companies a new philosophy towards training and development, one that mirrors the approach adopted by the talent led company in that they fully appreciate that training refines and develops talent, it doesn't create it. Equally in reviewing individual training requirements they must be fully cognizant of the fact that management can build on strengths and develop talents but cannot create them where they do not already exist. This fact appears to have escaped the attention of many in the personnel and training profession.

- Training needs to be seen as something we invest in rather than something we simply consume. Viewed in that way, measuring the return on that investment is a natural consequence rather than a minority activity. The pay off is that securing an adequate return means that training and development stops being the Cinderella of the budgetary process.

10

The Management Prescription

In Chapter 8 we defined the six basic problems facing organizations today as follows:-

- Widespread dissatisfaction with a lack of promotional opportunities and the consequential plateauing of careers.

- Lack of opportunity for individuals to develop their career from specialist functions to a generalist role.

- Managers wishing to exit from their current organizations to find a more challenging and fulfilling role.

- Other forms of employment eg, interim management, new business ventures, being viewed as more attractive than conventional careers.

- Dissatisfaction with current management development systems and the level of training provided.

- Insufficient regard to the real cost of high management turnover.

While instant solutions would, quite rightly, be seen as superficial, in the talent led organization the following approaches would be applied.

HELPING MANAGERS COME TO TERMS WITH ORGANIZATIONAL REALITY

First, part of the solution to the spectre of the growing disillusionment with corporate life can be remedied, as already discussed, by organizations pursuing imaginative reward and recognition policies and having soundly based promotion programmes and systems.

The problems arising from the down-sizing and plateauing of careers while being more difficult to address are not without solutions. As Scase and Goffee[1] describe 'some large corporations are attempting to retain the talents and energies of their managers by decentralizing their structures and encouraging the development of more autonomous management teams which are encouraged to be entrepreneurial'.

Effectively constructed and implemented, decentralization can be a powerful method of cascading through the organization the motivational effects of greater autonomy, responsibility, authority and accountability. However, it has to be for real – not illusory – and translate itself in varying degrees throughout the newly constituted operation or profit centre. Simply devolving greater autonomy to smaller trading companies or regional boards only provides part of the solution. They, in turn, need to devolve part of their greater autonomy to their management teams.

To this we can add the need for organizations to provide 'real' career counselling at the important career landmarks of, for example, 25 years, 35 years, 45 years. I use the word 'real' to distinguish this from the conventional performance review and to include the use of external professional career counsellors.

In addition, we can positively assist those individuals who are undergoing the stress of being passed over but for whom no real alternatives exist outside the organization, by helping them develop 'survival strategies'. In the UK, few companies provide this form of support, the net result being that such individuals will often experience emotional difficulties, family disharmony, impaired relationships with colleagues and so on, the net result being deteriorating performance before they come to terms with the situation – and some never do.

This is in sharp contrast to the USA where Employee Assistance Programmes (EAP) are common practice. The programmes provide employees with totally confidential access to external professional counsellors who provide advice and assistance in dealing with career problems, alcohol or drug dependency and so on. In the UK, concern as to the physical well-being of employees is well established, with company medical centres and provision of private medical insurance. The lesson perhaps is that in an increasingly stress filled world we need to give as much attention to the mental well-being of our employees.

FROM SPECIALIST TO GENERALIST

Second, we need to create more opportunities for individuals to change function within companies. It needs to become the norm rather than the exception for individuals to change from marketing, finance, personnel, to general management and vice versa.

In the talent led company it's not simply the functional experts progressing into general management; it's equally line management spending periods of their career heading up the functional disciplines such as finance, personnel, marketing and so on.

In contrast to the majority of British companies where the chief executive has either progressed from one of the functions (normally finance or marketing) or spent the whole of his career progressing through the line, in American corporations such individuals will have often spent periods of their career heading up a wide variety of both line and functional departments on their route to the top. There is, however, a growing realization by a number of UK companies that the manager of the 1990s will have to be multi-functional.

Based on a number of recruitment briefs being handled by the major head-hunters, the executive managers of the 1990s will have to demonstrate a track record of innovation, have a firm grasp of marketing, be as financially numerate as the finance director, and have a wide appreciation of the European dimension. As an example, Brian Gordon, northern managing director of Tyzack and Partners, sees a growing trend by client companies to concentrate on candidates who possess the skills that will meet their requirements over the next five years rather than relying on a proven track record that mirrors today's problems and opportunities.

For Mina Gouran, principal consultant with Heidrick & Struggles International, increasingly recruits are required to demonstrate an 'international awareness and the ability to do business at a pan-European level'. She maintains that this is still a requirement of companies predominantly operating in the UK market and, as such, demonstrates a growing awareness of the threat of European and international competition and the need for a 'cosmopolitan approach to business'. To this she would add 'hard evidence of commercial awareness irrespective of the function being recruited for'.

Companies that do not provide these opportunities will simply stimulate their most talented to discover them elsewhere.

PROVIDING CHALLENGE

Third, it must surely be a cause for concern that, in the Nicholson and West research, of the 17 responses elicited as to the reasons for the last job change the most quoted response was 'to do something

more challenging and fulfilling'. This problem is further compounded by the fact that the research indicated that the promotional
steps individuals make between companies are significantly greater
than those made by individuals who remain with their present
employer. Clearly the process of career planning and assessment of
potential needs to be more aspirational. That it is not, is an
illustration of the way our thinking has become conditioned by the
conventional organizational hierarchy with managers progressing up
the ladder of promotion one rung at a time. This approach is further
compounded by the majority of our management development
systems in that in assessing future potential we ask the reviewing
manager to 'identify the candidate's suitability for promotion to the
next grade or level in the organization'. We need to break out of
that cycle and appreciate that, in assessing future potential, some
individuals need to be developed and promoted one step at a time
and others have the capacity to make quantum leaps.

SETTING THE RIGHT ASPIRATIONS

Fourth, the fact that other forms of employment – interim management, new business ventures – are increasingly being seen as more
attractive than conventional careers, is of particular concern. Part
of the resolution to the problem was hinted at in the earlier
comments that have been made as to how we can positively
reward and recognize high performance in the business as well as
providing real career opportunities both within and across
functions. We need to establish a culture that understands and
practices the art of establishing the right aspirations for each and
every one of us.

One of the most important and yet most overlooked responsibili-
ties that management has is to create the right level of expectation
among subordinates. We set the standards in the organization either
directly or by default. People need to know what is expected of
them, and within sensible limits, the more stretching the goals are
the more individuals will aspire to meet and beat them. It's a simple
fact of life that *none of us is an achiever until someone expects
something of us*.

If the expectation matches our talent potential the net result is
that there is motivation and growth. If the expectation is wrong,
either too little or too much, we become bored or our performance
deteriorates. If you want to demoralize an individual, repeatedly

ask him or her to do something for which they have no adequate response in their repertoire of skills and abilities.

There will of course be a small number of individuals whose degree of self motivation is such that they need little or no stimulation from others to achieve their goals. They are however in a minority since, for must of us, talent develops in response to another individual. The aspirations, the expectations, the great people developers of life are capable of creating change in our belief in our ability to achieve from a flickering flame to a shining beacon.

MANAGEMENT DEVELOPMENT FOR REAL

Fifth, the dissatisfaction expressed by many managers about current management development systems and the level of training provided is not, as the current debate would have us believe, just about the quantity of training provided. Equally it is also about quality and the degree to which it does or does not enable individuals to cross functional boundaries. The benefit of seconding individuals to other departments and functions so that they can gain 'hands on' experience has been widely written on, but little practised in most organizations. The desire to avoid any interference with the day to day running of the business taking precedence over the long-term development of individuals. While a balance between the two has obviously to be struck we need, on occasions, to be more prepared to accept some organizational inconvenience in return for long-term growth in our staff.

Making your experience count

One of the positive results arising from the current debate on training is the recognition by the higher education authorities of the value of employees' existing experience and training in gaining academic awards. Credit Accumulation and Transfer Systems (CATS) is supported by the academic institutions, employers, the professions and career guidance services. Based on progress to date most individuals should be able to find a local university, polytechnic or college that can offer the opportunity of opting for CATS.[2]

In essence CATS is an alternative way of achieving academic awards. Instead of studying on a designated course, typically for three years full time, a student is able to negotiate their own programme from a range of courses and at a pace that suits the individual. To facilitate this, all course units are allocated a credit rating and there are a set number to be achieved for particular awards. A student accumulates selected credits towards the total number needed for that award. Furthermore, a student can transfer credits towards an award from previous studies including that from work-based activities, vocational qualifications or experiential learning. It is also possible for a student to study a CATS programme at more than one academic institution.

The prime reason for the development was the recognition that more students needed to be recruited to higher education from non-traditional backgrounds such as those with vocational qualifications or work experience. By providing credits for their previous learning and enabling them to accumulate further credits on a flexible basis, it was considered, quite rightly, that they would be attracted to higher education. Providing further flexibility through the facility for the negotiation of individually designed programmes has further added to the attraction of the CATS option.

Freeing up the education system in this way will not only attract a growing number of employees back into education and improve our skill base, it will also have a knock-on effect on the quality of internal company training programmes. If such internal training programmes are to be duly accredited by external academic bodies then the exposure of such programmes to external academic rigour should improve both their quality and focus.

Education and business partnership

Opening up higher education to market forces has also resulted in polytechnics and colleges being more responsive to the needs of industry. A number of them are now working in collaboration with companies in establishing training programmes which meet their needs, and on successful completion of the programmes, participants are awarded a recognized qualification.

One example from within Joshua Tetley is the diploma in Business Administration (DBA) partnered between the company and the Leeds Business School. In reviewing our training and development of managers it was felt that while our core training programme satisfied our primary training and education needs there was a requirement to improve further the skill base of our managers. The programme is open to all managers, with a maximum of 12 places a year and is conducted on a modular basis, the key topic areas being as follows:

- *Management information and control* – Concentrates on the importance of information as an organization resource, the best means of managing it, and the use of quantitative business skills. The module also introduces accounting terminology and financial decision making.

- *Marketing and economic analysis* – Seeks to teach the essentials of micro- and macro-marketing; the compilation, interpretation and use of marketing data and the complex relationship between economic, technical and social systems within a modern company.

- *The effective manager* – Related to the behavioural aspects of management, including individual and team motivational theories, group techniques and leadership skills, all in the context of greater personal effectiveness in working with, and managing, others.

- *Operations management* – Concerns the production operation in a company, its contribution to overall company profits and, in particular, the techniques used in managing a production operation.

The programme involves attendance at the Leeds Business School one day a week for three semesters, two weekend schools at which input is provided by both Business School and company personnel and a work based project.

On satisfactory completion individuals are awarded the Diploma in Business Administration, the credibility of the qualification being further enhanced by the fact that any candidate who achieves a pass rate of 60 per cent or more will be accepted by the School on their MBA programme. The opportunity for individuals to obtain recognized qualifications from pursuing such programmes is a powerful inducement for them as well as providing the company with a means of upgrading its managerial skill base.

Identifying your best people developers

Improving the quality of its management cadre is one of the key challenges facing British management today. There is no lack of debate on the subject, the need is for more positive action and commitment. We need to be aware of the executive who continually espouses the benefits of greater people development and training but in reality achieves very little. Such individuals can be described as the 'Italian manager – they have played to more galleries than Pavarotti'. If you want to discover how committed an individual is to training and development, just examine his track record; how many individuals have been promoted from his department? How many are in the company's future promotional plan?

Myron Rush[3], using a biblical reference, says that in James 1:22 we read 'Do not merely listen to the Word and so deceive ourselves. Do what it says'. He continues that 'to know and not apply is worse than not knowing'. Is it too unconventional to suggest that if the development of subordinates is to have a high priority in the organization then no individual should be promoted until he has identified a successor? Unconventional maybe, but that is the system that applies in Golden Corral, the American restaurant chain. Such a philosophy also impacts itself on selection in that managers do not set out to fill a vacancy but instead seek to appoint individuals with the talent to progress at least one step higher in the organization.

Equally, if employee development is to be at the top of the management agenda why not seek the opinions of members of staff as to how good a people developer their boss is. This too may be unorthodox, but that's the situation at Rank Xerox where managers are assessed by their staff. Those who do not achieve a 'role model' ranking are barred from the top 200 jobs in the company.

In a world where real managerial ability is always going to be in short supply, we need to use our selection, management development and training systems as the means by which we identify the untapped talent that lies largely undisturbed in most organizations. We need in particular to shake off some of the stereotypical images we possess. Are our stated requirements that candidates have to have a degree or other qualifications essential or just arbitrary? Since one can find little or no correlation between pure academic performance and business success the latter has to be the case, the essential truth being that its the possession of talent and the potential to develop that talent that is the key discriminator.

That raw talent is found in many guises. One such example is Janette Howgate who in 1982 was secretary to Joshua Tetley's Distribution Manager. In discussion she made it abundantly clear that she wished to do something more challenging and fulfilling and as a consequence she was advised to undertake the Certificate in Management Studies that the company was sponsoring in conjunction with the Wakefield College of Further Education. On completion of the course Janette was even more determined to pursue a career in management. Interviewed on our Area Manager structured interview we discovered that she had a whole range of talents relevant for a career in retail management. Commencing as a deputy area manager, within a year she was appointed area manager, four years in that post being followed by her appointment as retail regional manager responsible for a sales budget of £30 million and a team of 6 employees. Reflecting on her experience Janette says 'not many companies would give a secretary that opportunity or take that risk'. She adds 'it's worked out well for me and hopefully for the company'. Janette is currently in her final year of the MBA programme.

A further clue to identifying the best people developers is the degree to which they delegate responsibility to their subordinates. For the natural developer coaching subordinates and obtaining satisfaction at seeing how they grow from the experience of being more accountable and having delegated decision making authority is part of every day life. The high developer gives individuals whole jobs to do, guiding them at the margin, allowing them to experience the learning that results from both success and making the odd mistake. In contrast, the low developer gives people individual tasks to do, the net result being that subordinates never fully appreciate their part in the total jigsaw. For the high developer delegation is a natural style since he or she instinctively understands that the end result of delegation is the opportunity for individuals to make significant choices. In making those choices subordinates can discover *the feeling of ownership* – this is mine to do, I must do it well.

Building better relationships

Equally, effective managers take time out to build sound productive relationships with their staff. They understand that how people feel about their boss is probably the single most important determinant of how much they are prepared to contribute to the company. How many times have we heard the expression 'I could work for that guy' or the reverse? Good managers seek out opportunities to invest time in their staff, see them as team players and almost certainly experience high morale and low staff turnover. John Garnett, the former Director of the Industrial Society was once asked at a conference 'do you have to like the people who work for you?' John paused and replied 'No, you don't have to like the people who work for you – you are paid to love them'.

Training can be a powerful agent in cementing sound relationships.

It will be recalled that in Part 1 we highlighted the fact that turnover of bar staff had declined from 148 per cent to 97 per cent as a consequence of the use of structured interviews at Joshua Tetley. To test the effect of training in improving manager/staff relationships a pilot study of 14 of our large pubs was undertaken. Each of the managers selected undertook the three-day Craft Trainer Award training programme which is validated by the Hotel and Catering Training Company. The programme is designed to enable managers to undertake effective one to one training of their staff. Six months after completion of the training, staff turnover had declined from 97 per cent to 68 per cent, and six months on had further fallen to 63 per cent.

THE REAL COST OF LABOUR TURNOVER

The sixth and final point arising from the Nicholson and West research is the need for better management of the job change process and greater regard for the real cost of labour turnover.

Induction – are they left to sink or swim?

As a source of learning during the initial joining period, company literature and in-company induction training was roundly condemned by the participants in that research, with over 70 per cent describing them as 'virtually useless'. It is accordingly difficult to escape the conclusion that, in the majority of companies, despite spending large sums on recruiting and attracting managers into the organization once they join they are 'left to sink or swim in the deep end'.

This lack of suitable induction training can only result in loss of effective management time, with a consequential cost penalty, as the individual struggles to come to terms with working for his new employer. Equally, ineffective induction into the organization increases the risk of individuals leaving, since most surveys of labour turnover illustrate that the greatest incidence of turnover occurs during the first three to six months of employment. In the service sector the period can be as short as a week. The handling of new entrants, their transition and adjustment to the new working environment, needs to move up the personnel agenda. Well designed and constructed induction programmes need to involve the most senior members of the management team. In very large organizations it can often present one of the few opportunities for junior staff to meet key executives face to face. Furthermore, it gives management the opportunity to explain at first hand the company's style, it's culture, it's future plans, all before the cynics in the organization get to work.

Employees leave managers not companies

We also need to understand better the cost to the organization of high labour turnover. I am continually amazed at the number of personnel/human resource departments which do not systematically track staff turnover. When they do, few convert that turnover into its potential effects on the bottom line profit of the organization. David Bainton, principal associate at Coopers and Lybrand, gives examples of the cost of labour turnover as follows:

- Cost of replacing a computer sales person: £170,000 (IBM).

- Cost of replacing a cashier: £9–10,000 (building societies).

- Cost of training a nurse: £30,000 (NHS).

Within Joshua Tetley the basic cost of replacing a licensee is estimated at £3000 and a member of barstaff at £450. Based on current staff turnover rates, that represents a potential bottom line cost of £450,000 for licensee turnover and £2,600,000 for bar staff turnover. Put in those terms, staff turnover rates become a serious subject for debate within the organization.

The costs of labour turnover detailed above are significant in themselves but in the hospitality industry a further factor comes into play – customer loyalty. It is not unknown, after all, for exceptionally good bar staff to attract customers to their new venue. While it is difficult to be precise as to the real cost to the business let us try a simple example related to a regular pub user. Based on six visits a week and the purchase of four pints per visit the weekly spend will be around £30. With a customer lifetime of approximately ten years, the potential value is £15,600.

Since one of the endearing qualities of the British pub is that people meet in groups or congregate with friends, when a regular leaves to go to a new venue he will normally take up to three others with him. Therefore the real potential cost of losing that regular becomes not four pints a night but £15,600 × 4 or £62,400. Since all companies have regular customers the selection and retention of quality staff needs to be top of the management agenda of every organization that is involved in selling either products or services, and any company that doesn't come into one or both of those definitions must be pretty unique. Add to the cost debate the forecast demographic changes in the employment structure within the UK and no one should be surprised by the prediction that in the future departmental managers will discover that *staff turnover rates assume as high a priority as departmental profit and loss accounts.*

The real reasons employees leave

If we are to appreciate the nature of the problem of labour turnover then we have to understand why individuals join us and then subsequently leave. For those companies that conduct exit interviews, the way the interview is carried out in the majority of situations leaves more than a little to be desired. It is usually conducted as a general chat with both parties anxious to avoid embarrassing encounters. Once the fact that the person is leaving to take up a job that pays more is revealed the assumption is made that this is the fundamental reason for departure and both parties can get back to wishing each other well for the future, whether sincerely meant or not. Checking on the most common response, more pay, can lead to some interesting answers, for it is not unusual for the level of increased pay to be relatively small or in fact for there to be no actual pay increase at all. It is often simply the case of an individual appreciating that it is socially more acceptable to give that reason than the true facts influencing his or her departure.

One way of better understanding the reasons for individuals leaving is to conduct a structured exit interview using a set of predetermined questions. The interview can be conducted on a face to face basis or over the telephone, either in the last week of employment or after the individual has left. Our own research indicated that there is no difference in the level of frankness exhibited whichever method is adopted.

Based on a sample of 100 exit interviews of pub managers the answers (overleaf) in rank order (1 being the most quoted) to a sample of the questions asked is revealing.

A more illuminating set of answers than the cliche response, more pay. While those responses are based on a limited sample of only 100 it does provide some supportive evidence to the research referred to earlier, as well as supporting some of the assertions made on the basis of practical day to day experience.

Question	Rank order % of respondents
Why did you join Tetleys?	
Company reputation	1
Career opportunity	2
Opportunity for me and my partner to work together	3
Salary	4
How long did you work with Tetleys?	
1–6 months	1
8–12 months	2
2–3 years	3
4–5 years	4
Why have you decided to leave?	
Area manager	1
Better business opportunity	2
Domestic reasons	3
Salary	4
How would you describe your relationship with your area manager?	
Poor	70%
Good	20%
Excellent	10%
Was your area manager interested in your career development?	
Yes	13%
No	87%

Explain more about your relationship with your Manager
Sample responses
- She was not interested in our career progression – we felt we were just being used.
- He acted as a policeman – he was only interested in the weekly takings, not in us.
- We rarely saw him.

Did you enjoy your work?	
Yes	100%
No	0%

In your opinion were you successful?

Yes	90%
No	10%

What motivated you towards success?

Personal goals	1
Customers	2
Recognition } equal third	3
Career	3
Salary	4
Bonus	5

How did you measure your success?

Customers	1
Take	2
Controllable profit	3
Stocks	4

Would you ever work for Tetley's again?

Yes	90%
No	10%

Highlighting the problems of staff turnover during a period of recession might at first sight seem odd, particularly as some organizations see encouraging higher turnover as a means of painlessly and cost effectively reducing the headcount. The danger for such organizations it that very often *it is the best people who leave the worst organizations first*. Equally we need to appreciate that *most employees leave managers, not companies*.

As I have outlined the two final components of the talent equation are creating and satisfying employee expectations and positively investing in their medium- and long-term growth. The link between this and the previous section which focused on reward and recognition is the fact that in the words of Michael Armstrong

the most important thing to remember about performance management is that it is a continuous process shared between managers and the people for whom they are responsible. It is concerned both with improving results and with the quality of working relationships.[4]

The challenge for organizations today, more than ever before, is to provide a culture in which individuals can attain self expression, achievement and fulfillment from work. The key components of that culture include positively influencing individual goals and expectations, having sound promotional policies and investing adequate resources into training and development. Pursuing that philosophy will enable organizations better to appreciate that, in an age of uncertainty, the people we employ are the only true means by which we can achieve a sustainable competitive advantage over our rivals.

SUMMARY

In this chapter we have concluded that:

- We need to ensure that our management development systems, our manpower planning processes and the way in which we organize and structure our companies are compatible with maximizing challenge and satisfaction from work.

- Our manpower planning and development systems need consciously to provide opportunities whereby crossing functional boundaries becomes the norm, not the exception.

- If we believe that the development of employees is of significance to our future well-being as an organization, then we need to identify and recognize our best people developers.

- We need better understanding of the real reasons employees leave and determine the cost to the organization of high labour turnover. The cost calculation must include both the direct and indirect effects internally and externally on our customer base.

REFERENCES

1 Scase, R and Goffee, R (1989) *Reluctant Managers* Unwin Hyman, London.
2 'Opting for CATS', *Newscheck with Careers Service Bulletin* vol 1, no 10, May 1991.
3 Rush, M (1983) *Management: A Biblical Approach* SP Publications, Maryland, USA.
4 Armstrong, M (1977) *A Handbook of Personnel Management Practice* Kogan Page, London.

THE SEVEN ISSUES FOR THE BOARD AGENDA

1. Produce a clear, strong mission statement which enables employees to relate to, and identify with, the company's goals and objectives.

2. Consciously communicate the company's vision through the management team and ensure that their day to day activities and company policies and philosophies are in accord with that vision.

3. Promulgate a management style that enables the organization to get the best out of the people it employs.

4. Audit the organization's promotion policies – discover whether we are promoting the 'effective' or the 'successful' manager.

5. Consistently measure the impact of training on the key performance indices the company values, and then debate whether we are investing sufficient resources in this area.

6. Establish the effect on company profitability of labour turnover and regularly review areas of high turnover.

7. Give as much 'air time' to evaluating the impact of human resource activities on the company's profit performance as to income and cost statements.

▶ PART 4 ◀

Customers – the Talent Connection

11

The Consumer Rules

As we said in the introduction the initial reaction of organizations seeking to achieve a competitive advantage has been to embark on quality and service initiatives. The key to converting that advantage into a sustainable competitive advantage is to apply such initiatives in an environment where the talent formula is practised as a way of life. The essential link between the talent formula and quality of service is that customer service initiatives are no substitute for sound management and personnel policies and philosophies, in reality they are a mandatory pre-requisite for an effective programme.

In terms of an historical perspective to this subject, for a nation that once prided itself on being the workshop of the world, leading innovation and being a by-word for quality, the reality over the last 30 years or so has been a continued deterioration in markets where British goods were once dominant. In the domestic market the pride of place that used to be reserved in the shop windows of the high street for British manufactured goods has been taken by foreign imports. The exhortations of those organizations so reminiscent of the 1960s and 1970s to 'buy British' failed not through lack of appreciation by the buying public that purchasing foreign goods meant importing unemployment, but simply because imported goods represented better value for money. Better value for money not simply in terms of cost but product innovation, reliability and so on.

There was also a failure by companies during this period to recognise a growing consumer awareness and greater sophistication in the public's purchasing habits. As Tony McBurnie and David Clutterbuck argue:

> The plain fact is that if even half of the major (let alone the minor) companies in Britain understood and reacted to customers' needs as well as they should, the entire economy would be far stronger than it is now – and the Japanese would be trooping here to find out how it was done.[1]

Marketing functions in a whole variety of organizations have become obsessed with producing torrents of data relating to brand share, product distribution, competitor analysis, television ratings and so on. While few would argue against the view that this is important information, the argument in favour is diminished when, as so often happens, it is produced at the expense of consumer research. Losing touch with changing markets and failing to understand the shifts in consumer needs have been major factors in influencing the decline and failure of a number of companies. As Peters and Waterman propound 'Markets do not buy anything – customers do'.[2] That large sections of the British manufacturing base have been slow to respond to consumer requirements is beyond dispute, but the combination of foreign competition and the influence of the retailer acting on behalf of the consumer is forcing change.

As Peter Herriot observes 'A core competence of the retailer is to be able to discover and react to the demands of the consumer'.[3] The influence of the high street retailers and suppliers has been far reaching in its impact not only on the fast moving consumer goods market, but also on manufacturing in general and the mass of service providers. Furthermore, as the high street has become more responsive to consumer needs in improving service levels, paying greater attention to design and decor, the creation of shopping ambience etc, so too have they become a potent force in driving up consumers' expectations at large.

The improved standard of service we experience in the high street, we now expect in all our transactions as customers. No longer are we prepared to be tolerant of poor service and quality, be it from public utilities or the private sector.

Acceptance of the fact that consumerism has become a reality of survival, has led to an explosion in the number of companies throughout the UK introducing customer service campaigns. Expectations were high, with many claiming that this was the single most important initiative in creating a sustainable competitive advantage. Whilst few would argue with the sentiment that improved customer service can have a marked effect on sales, customer retention and improved profitability, has reality matched those expectations?

WHY CUSTOMER SERVICE INITIATIVES FAIL

David Clutterbuck, Chairman of the Item Group and an experienced commentator on customer service initiatives, estimates that 'up to 90 per cent of the programmes in existence have either failed, or will fail in the near future'. The arguments to support that view include the following factors in a number of companies:

- 'There is almost a total absence of clear objectives to support the initiative'. In addition, there has been a marked failure to measure the level of service and product quality currently experienced compared with the level to which the organization is aspiring.

- 'The customer service programme was very often born out of desperation – the, we've tried everything else, syndrome'. The initiative is seen as an organizational quick fix rather than a way of life requiring a long-term commitment.

- 'A significant number of the programmes are the product of bought-in prescriptive package solutions which are too inflexible to be owned by both managers and employees'.

- Insufficient regard has been taken of the fact that becoming customer service driven requires a different management style; 'the abandonment of the traditional controlling style of management (in which subordinates are there to help the manager do his job) in favour of an enabling style (in which the manager is here to help his subordinates do their job of satisfying customer needs)'.

To this Tom Peters[4] adds 'Most quality programmes fail for one of two reasons: 'They have systems without passion, or passion without systems. You must have both'.

The benefits of doing it right

Despite the inherent difficulties in establishing an effective customer service and product quality programme, the potential returns on doing it well are highly seductive. Surveys suggest that high service driven companies are able to charge up to 9 per cent more for the goods and services they offer. They grow twice as fast as the average and have the potential to gain up to 6 per cent more market share, a powerful economic argument for being simply the best customer service driven company in your market sector.

Equally, poor service has a real cost penalty. It costs up to five times as much to go out and get a new customer as to retain those you have. Or, as Robert Desatnick, former corporate vice-president of McDonald's puts it, 'the cost of losing a repeat customer is approximately five times the value of that annual account'.

Despite this, British companies continue to spend literally tens of millions of pounds seeking to attract new customers through advertising and promotional campaigns while, at the same time, being seemingly totally oblivious to the fact that established customers are haemorrhaging through the back door. This is in marked contrast to the situation at Mercedes who have an impressive 85 per cent repeat purchase level.

THE COST OF THE DISSATISFIED CUSTOMER

In today's increasingly competitive marketplace it is obvious that it's the customer who decides which company succeeds and which loses. Evidence to support that assertion is provided by TARP (Technical Assistant Research Programmes) based on research carried out in the USA and Canada over several years into the benefits of good customer relations. In the research they surveyed over 200 companies and organizations ranging from Coca Cola to the White House.

They found that:

- Most dissatisfied customers do not complain. The average business does not hear from 96 per cent of it's unhappy customers.

- For every complaint received there will be another 26 customers with problems, at least 6 of these will be serious.

- Complaints are often not made at all because people think it's not worth the time and effort, they don't know how or where to complain, or they believe the company would be indifferent to them.

- Non-complainers are the least likely group to buy from the company again. A complainer who gets a response is more likely to come back. Between 65 per cent and 90 per cent of non-complainers will never buy from the company again and the company will never know why.

- A company should welcome complaints as a second chance to keep a customer.

- Even a complaint made but not satisfactorily dealt with makes the customer 10 per cent more likely to come back – just being able to complain helps.

- When customers complain and the matter is dealt with satisfactorily 54 per cent will buy again. If the complaint is dealt with quickly and efficiently the retention rate rises to 90–95 per cent (these figures refer to major purchases such as domestic appliances, a motor car or an insurance policy).

- For smaller purchases such as food items, clothes or household goods 37 per cent of unhappy non-complainers will not purchase again; 82 per cent of complainers will purchase again if their complaint is handled well.

- Damage may not be restricted to the person with a complaint. A customer who has had an unpleasant experience will tell an average of nine or ten other people. Of those with a complaint 13 per cent will tell more than 20 others.

- When a complainer has received a satisfactory response he or she will tell only half the number of people and will talk about it positively.

Further evidence on consumer attitudes and perception in the UK can be found in research commissioned by the Office of Fair Trading into 'Consumer Loyalty' (published in May 1990). The main finding of the research, undertaken by Research Surveys of Great Britain, parallelled those of similar surveys conducted in America.

Despite the inherent difficulties in maintaining an effective customer service campaign, a number of well known individuals and companies within the UK can be identified as truly committed to 'putting the customer first'. While obviously not exhaustive, the list would include such names as Anita Roddick of Body Shop, Lord Rayner of Marks & Spencer, Clive Thompson of Rentokill, Alan Cathcart of Avis, Richard Branson of Virgin, and so on. This is a diverse range of individuals and companies but with one common purpose, a dedication to being the best providers of customer service in their market sector; companies that provide role models as we seek to commit our organizations to being the best providers of service and quality in our own market sector.

SUMMARY

In this chapter we concluded that:

- We need to ensure that throughout the organization there is a full appreciation and acceptance of the direct relationship between quality and service and the ability to secure a competitive advantage. That advantage can only be converted into a sustainable competitive one within the talent led organization.

- By being aware of the four most common reasons why customer service initiatives fail we will ensure that we avoid those problem areas or take appropriate remedial action.

- The cost/benefit research as to the impact of good and poor service on consumer perceptions and attitude and ultimately on company performance is a powerful reinforcement of the fundamental importance of quality and service.

- Customer service initiatives are no substitute for soundly based management and personnel policies and philosophies.

REFERENCES

1 McBurnie, T and Clutterbuck, D (1989) *The Marketing Edge*, Weidenfeld and Nicholson, London.
2 Peters, T and Waterman, R H (1981) *In Search Of Excellence*, Harper and Row, New York.
3 Herriot, P (1992) *The Career Management Challenge*, Sage, London.
4 Peters, T (1988) *Thriving On Chaos*, Macmillan, London.

12

'Cheers' – the Joshua Tetley Experience

It was as a consequence of changing public attitudes and expectations that Joshua Tetley decided to review and reappraise it's approach to quality and service. In terms of consumer perception, of all the traditions of the British way of life, probably few are greeted with more affection than the British pub. However, unlike most venerable institutions, its survival has been based on it's ability to adjust to changing consumer tastes and values.

The tranquil picture of 'mine host' so beloved of journalists and customers alike, belies the tremendous changes that have taken place in the industry as companies have sought to gain a competitive edge over their rivals. Throughout the 1970s and 1980s the brewing industry invested heavily in new plant and technology, as it came to terms with consumers' demands for a consistent, high quality product and the growing lager market. It also had to come to terms with the fact that in a more affluent and health conscious society, it no longer held a privileged position in consumer spending. The brewing industry had to compete with a whole host of markets for it's share of the leisure pound.

The revolution in the British high street not only increased the pressure on consumers' disposable income, but also fundamentally changed consumers' expectations as they experienced greatly improved service levels and the shopping ambience created by imaginative design and decor. The reality is that those standards and expectations now form the benchmark against which customer's measure what we offer. It was in response to those changing consumer expectations that brewing companies considerably increased the level of investment in major pub refurbishment programmes. They also had to come to terms with the need to segment their market into outlets catering for specific age groups, activity interests and the growing market for pub food.

While these changes were generally welcomed by the consumer, it became apparent that simply concentrating on product quality and an enhanced drinking environment would only yield a short-run advantage over the competition. The reality is that new pub concepts, improved design and decor can quickly be replicated by the competition. Furthermore, brewing technology and quality control systems have reached the stage where any deviation from product specification can quickly be corrected.

It was against this background that Joshua Tetley concluded that the only way to achieve a real, substantial competitive edge was to commit the company to becoming a service-driven organization. It was also felt that the climate of employee morale and commitment was at a level whereby a customer service programme would be positively received.

BUILDING THE FOUNDATIONS

As will be recalled from earlier chapters the company, building on the new employee relations climate created during the early 1980s, had pursued a number of initiatives:

- Overhauled its payment systems. The essential proposition being what happens in organizations is what you reward.

- Improved its methods of communication and consultation. The key thrust being to put the responsibility for communication where it belongs – line management.

- Invested more resources into training and development, not simply to raise the quality of its management stock, but in recognition of the fact that in a labour market that will become increasingly talent driven, individuals will be able to choose the companies they want on their curriculum vitae.

- Reviewed its selection systems. The prime focus being on the recruitment of talent through structured interviews modelled on the best performers in that employment group.

- Achieved a more equitable balance in the power relationship with the trade unions.

All of the above are essential steps in providing the structure, the framework from within which quality and service can flourish.

Quality and service starts from within

It was against that background that Joshua Tetley introduced it's 'Quality Pays' programme. The company had previously had a number of flirtations with the subject and during 1986 introduced a customer care training programme that centred on employees at the customer interface – the 'sharp end' of the business. This involved training for our pub managers and bar staff in improving service to the customer, as well as training for our delivery crews to stress the importance of customer deliveries being handled courteously and in the planned time.

All 'good stuff' but after several months of courses and motivational sessions we appeared to be making little progress that could be measured or quantified. What we did hear from time to time was: 'Why should I be bothered to give good service to my customers when I don't get it either for myself or my staff'.

That point was graphically brought home to me one night when I was visiting one of our pubs. On asking the licensee how the customer care training programme was going, he appeared less than enthusiastic. Since this was a manager who had originally been one of the most committed adherents to the programme I pushed him further. 'Well' he said, 'during this afternoon I held a training session for the staff on how we are going to improve the level of service we give to our customers, and then at five o'clock this afternoon I get a 'phone call from the brewery to say that the staff wages are not available due to a problem with the computer'.

Or the delivery crew who after attending a training session on improving customer service return to their vehicle to find that several product lines are not available due to a production planning problem. Isolated examples maybe, but those comments and situations have important strategic implications in that, whilst its important to improve the level of quality and service at the customer interface, such initiatives are never going to be truly effective until we are all able to give excellent service to each other within the organization.

THE QUALITY PAYS PROGRAMME

It was from that philosophy that the Joshua Tetley 'Quality Pays' programme evolved. To assist us in the delivery of the programme, we used the services of Lifeskills Associates, a Leeds-based consultancy specializing in customer service initiatives. Lifeskills was chosen because, first, they were specialists in this particular area. Second, for them, quality and service is an emotion, not just a mechanistic intellectual exercise, and therefore they were able to provide both passion and a systematic approach.

Furthermore, we needed to develop an infrastructure that facilitated 'Quality Pays' as an on-going process. That is vital; Organizations that simply hold a one-off event to emphasize quality and service, irrespective of how inspirational it is or how much glitz they import, will fail. All they achieve, in practice, is to raise short-term aspirations and create long-term disillusionment.

The programme had three basic aims:

1. Establishment of service teams – groups of up to 20 employees, headed by the appropriate line manager or supervisor, coming together about once a month.
2. Introduction of a 12-module programme from which the service teams would discuss together how they would improve the level of service they provide – both internally within the department and to their customers within and outside the business. The 12 steps comprised of:
   - Deciding What Business We Are In.
   - Knowing Our Customers.
   - Create Our Vision.
   - Identify Our Moments Of Truth.
   - Give Good Service To Each Other.
   - Creating The Customers Experience – People Skills.
   - Creating The Customers Experience – The Product.
   - Creating The Customers Experience – Packaging.
   - Creating The Customers Experience – Practices.
   - Profit From Complaints.
   - Setting Service Standards.
   - Stay Close To Our Customers.
3. The formation of a company steering group composed of a representative number of executive directors, managers and employees. The role of the steering group was to monitor progress, review training requirements, act as a sounding board for the service teams, and be a vehicle by which their overall views and opinions could be communicated to the Board. The steering group, or such co-ordinating body, is not designed to manage or oversee the day to day activities of the service teams, that is a line management responsibility. That in some companies the steering group assumes this role is to the detriment of the whole programme in that it leads to line management abdicating their responsibility with a consequential loss of involvement in, and commitment to, the programme.

Training and involvement for all

The training programme to support the initiative involved:

1. A four day Service Team Leader Workshop, attended by the 100 service team leaders, plus all directors and senior management. The inclusion of the whole executive management team, whether they were involved in actually running service teams or not, was deliberate. It is critical for the management team to share a common philosophy and common language.
2. A series of 14 one-day workshops on quality and service, attended by everyone throughout the organization in groups of 150. The groups were organized to represent a cross-section of functions and status throughout the organization, thereby avoiding the predictable reaction: 'My group is in step – the problem is the other departments'.

PERCEPTIONS AND ATTITUDES

Whilst the logistics of involving everyone throughout the organization in 14 continuous one-day programmes was formidable it was a necessary prerequisite if the initiative was to be ultimately successful. Employee fears that they were going to be subjected to a day of classroom style lectures were quickly disabused as they saw that the whole day was to be focused on a minimum input from the Lifeskills training staff and a maximum amount of group discussion and feedback; this process being in keeping with Lifeskills philosophy of training – 'why teach people things they can discover for themselves?'

A programme of this nature involving 2000 employees provides a tremendous amount of data, and despite a lack of scientific precision is a useful guide to the attitudes and perceptions that are prevalent in an organization. As part of the exercise people were split into 200 groups of ten and asked 'What are we good at?' and the reverse side of the coin: 'What could we be better at?' Out of the total maximum score of 200 (number of times mentioned) under the heading of 'What are we good at?' employee group response was as follows:

1. Public relations, sponsorship and community relations (153 mentions).
2. Brewing high quality beer (150 mentions with 44 groups extending the questions into 'applauding a good product range').

3. Looking after employees, including good working conditions, benefits, care of pensioners (125).
4. Customer awareness, including preserving the Tetley tradition (120).
5. Range and standard of pubs (117).
6. Selection, training and development of employees (90).

These six responses topped the strengths list. The reverse 'What could we be better at?' resulted in the following views from the 200 groups:

1. Improving internal communications (183 mentions).
2. More reward and recognition for good performers (145).
3. More effective advertising and marketing (132).
4. Better teamwork/integration between departments (102).
5. More staff training and development (100).
6. Request for more visibility of senior management (78).

As the strengths list indicated employees were generally satisfied with the quality of training provided, what was being identified was a 'hunger for more'.

As will be recalled from earlier chapters a number of steps have been progressively taken by the company to remedy the areas of concern identified by employees. However, all in all, compared with similar exercises conducted in a variety of other organizations the Tetley results can be judged to be more than satisfactory. The desire to achieve continual improvement is the hallmark of companies aspiring to be talent led. After all *you don't have to be ill to want to be better.*

MEASURING THE IMPACT – THE INTERNAL CUSTOMER

Three years into our Quality Pays programme we can say that we have substantially raised the level of awareness and consciousness of everyone in the organization to the importance of quality and service. The results of our internal attitude surveys indicate that the programme enjoys the support and commitment of the majority of our employees. Of fundamental importance is the requirement to measure what is currently being experienced compared with the level to which the organization is aspiring. Employee attitude is one measurement among many that falls within that definition and is arguably one of the most important. As Philip Atkinson[1] says 'Effective customer service is based upon changing the attitudes of "boundary personnel", the people who come into contact with customers'.

Based upon the PA Management Consultancy employee attitude survey the following 20 questions were constructed, employees being asked to indicate where in their view the company lay between the two statements.

QUESTIONNAIRE

I should be grateful if you would complete the following questionnaire by circling the number that, in your view, reflects where we are between the two opposing statements.

1. The company's concern is to maximize profits at the expense of quality and customer service.

   Management are committed to increasing profits through improved quality and customer service.

   | 1 | 2 | 3 | 4 | 5 |

2. Management are always busy with reports, budgets, monthly returns, etc. and are rarely seen.

   Management regularly talk to employees and listen to their views about quality and customer service.

   | 1 | 2 | 3 | 4 | 5 |

3. Employees are not interested in contributing to improving customer service.

   Management regularly encourage employees to contribute to improving customer service.

   | 1 | 2 | 3 | 4 | 5 |

4. Maximizing profit is the sole objective of departments.

   Every department's goal is increasing profit through improved quality and service.

   | 1 | 2 | 3 | 4 | 5 |

5. Quality is about producing the perfect pint.

   Quality is about continually satisfying all of our customers' requirements.

   | 1 | 2 | 3 | 4 | 5 |

6. Only our pubs have customers.   Every department in the company has customers.

  •   •

1	2	3	4	5

7. Maintaining and improving quality is the responsibility of management.   Maintaining and improving quality is a key part of everybody's job.

  •   •

1	2	3	4	5

8. Quality improvement is a costly exercise.   Improving quality reduces costs.

  •   •

1	2	3	4	5

9. Some errors and defects are acceptable.   Error-free work is the only acceptable standard.

  •   •

1	2	3	4	5

10. Errors are detected by control systems and then put right.   It is everyone's responsibility to detect and correct errors in their work.

  •   •

1	2	3	4	5

11. Waste is identified as scrap, excess material, etc.   Waste is any activity which does not help towards improving customer service.

  •   •

1	2	3	4	5

12. The employee's role is to work to his job description and follow management instructions.   The majority of employees are committed to being members of a team that strives to improve quality and customer service.

  •   •

1	2	3	4	5

13. Departments are mainly concerned with improving efficiency and protecting themselves from criticism.   Departments work together to satisfy the customer.

  •   •

1	2	3	4	5

14. Employees are trained until they possess the necessary skills to cope with their jobs.
  •

Employees are continuously trained to develop their potential.
  •

1	2	3	4	5

15. Employees are mainly judged on their volume of work.
  •

Employees are mainly judged on the quality of their work.
  •

1	2	3	4	5

16. The company does not listen and respond to the requirements of customers.
  •

The company listens to its customers and acts positively to satisfy their demands.
  •

1	2	3	4	5

17. Company profitability does not depend on the level of customer satisfaction.
  •

Satisfied customers ensure a more profitable and secure company.
  •

1	2	3	4	5

18. The company does not adequately recognize employees who give good customer service.
  •

The company positively recognizes individuals who promote good customer service.
  •

1	2	3	4	5

19. The manager/supervisor's role is to instruct and supervise employees.
  •

The manager/supervisor's role is to coach and support his team.
  •

1	2	3	4	5

20. The quality and service provided to our customers remains constant.
  •

The company is continually seeking to improve the quality and service to its customers.
  •

1	2	3	4	5

Whilst anonymity of reply is guaranteed, for the purpose of analysis would you please tick the box which applies:

1. Your current department   **2. Job Group**

Distribution	Hourly paid employee
Production	Clerical & Grades 1–4A staff
Engineering	Management
Retail/Tenancy	
Free Trade	
Finance	
Admin	
Estates/TTS/Protection Services Marketing/Personnel	
Depots	

THANK YOU FOR COMPLETING THE QUESTIONNAIRE

In evaluating the results of the survey the indicators provided by PA were reconstructed as follows:

75–100
Congratulations! Yours is a quality company. But do not rest on your laurels. Quality is a continuous process. You need to be thinking about tomorrow's improvements today.

50–74
Your company is well above average for Europe. But you still have to convince people in your organization of the need for a continuous improvement in quality and service.

25–49
If your quality costs are not keeping you awake at night, then you probably haven't a clear enough idea of what they are. Your company is uncomfortably vulnerable to competitors who do take quality seriously.

20–24

It's a miracle you are still in business. Your lack of attention to quality makes you a prime target for quality-conscious competitors.

The scores achieved in the Joshua Tetley surveys were:

1987	56
1989	64
1991	71

Further information on employee perceptions is available by subdividing the questions asked in the survey into three headings, Quality, Service and Management Style. Comparing the responses in 1991 with those obtained in 1989, the improvements in those areas were:

Quality	+9%
Service	+9%
Management Style	+21%

MEASURING THE IMPACT – THE EXTERNAL CUSTOMER

Independent surveys of our external customers as to how the quality of our products and the level of service we provide compares with our competitors continues to show an improvement on the levels achieved prior to the programme being introduced. No one of course can, or would want to, claim that these improvements are solely due to the Quality Pays programme. They are a consequence of a number of factors, not least the dedicated efforts of individual pub licensees and their staff, the retail management team and production and distribution personnel, but nevertheless there is an interesting correlation between the two.

The surveys collect drinkers' opinions on beer quality, atmosphere and how well the pub is maintained among the five major breweries in Yorkshire. Their views are expressed in ratings on a one to five scale, one being top. Information is gathered every three months by an independent market research company interviewing hundreds of households where people visit pubs regularly.

In 1988 Joshua Tetley's ranked position, on a scale of one to five was as follows:

	Rank
Good Beer	2
Good Atmosphere	3
Well Maintained	5

In 1990 it had risen to:

	Rank
Good Beer	1
Good Atmosphere	1
Well Maintained	2

SUMMARY

In this chapter we concluded that:

- A substantial competitive advantage can be established through becoming a service and quality driven company.

- Quality and service has to start within the organization and until we are able to give consistently good service to each other we will never materially improve the level at the customer interface.

- Maintaining the quality and service momentum requires companies to develop an infrastructure within which the programme can exist.

- Training should involve everyone in the organization in order that there is a shared philosophy and common language.

- We need to consistently measure the impact of the programme on our external customers and employees alike.

REFERENCES

1. Atkinson, P (1990) *Creating Culture Change*, IFS Publications.

13

Six Ingredients for Being the Best

From our experience in Joshua Tetley over the last three years we would suggest that six key ingredients can be distilled which enable companies to mount and maintain effective quality and service initiatives.

COMMITMENT FROM THE TOP

To be truly effective, customer service campaigns have to be owned by top management. The stimulus for successful initiatives may come from personnel or marketing, but, to be truly successful, they have to be owned intellectually, psychologically and physically by the chief executive. CEOs provide the role models for everyone throughout the organization. Their commitment is seen, despite all the day to day pressures they face, by how much time they personally allocate to meeting customers and staff at the 'sharp end'.

The fact that Pete Harman, chief executive of Harman Stores, the largest Kentucky Fried Chicken concessionaire in America, spends 50 per cent of his working time talking to staff and listening to customers is a positive endorsement of his commitment.

Equally, Tom Farmer of Kwik-Fit not only visits each of his depots on a regular basis, but also commits one evening a fortnight to telephoning customers to enquire how they had found the service the previous day.

But you may well ask whether we can take top management commitment for granted? Evidence to clearly suggest we cannot is provided by Colin Coulson-Thomas[1] in his survey of directors and senior executives in over 100 organizations with a combined turnover of some £85 billion and 1.6 billion employees. The participants in this study, which was sponsored by ODI International, were asked to attach varying degrees of significance to selected barriers to the successful implementation of a quality process. The overall ranking of the barriers, in terms of 'very significant' replies, was as shown in Table 13.1.

Table 13.1 Quality barriers ranked according to number of 'very significant' replies

Barrier	%
Top management commitment	92
Too narrow an understanding of quality	38
Horizontal boundaries between functions and specialisms	31
Vested interests	29
Organizational politics	28
Cynicism	28
Organizational structure	27
Customer expectations	26
Speed of corporate action	24
Too general an approach	18
Loss of momentum	17
Boredom	15
Gap between management expectation/process achievement	15
Vendors'/suppliers' capabilities	15
Subsidiary/parent relationships	9
Cost	6

Source: Coulson-Thomas, C

AN INTEGRAL PART OF BUSINESS STRATEGY

Secondly, quality and service has to be an integral part of the business strategy, it cannot be seen in isolation from the key business decision activities. In the most successful companies, decisions on production planning, operating systems, new product development, and financial and administrative controls are made from the standpoint of 'Does it enhance quality and service?'

Despite the growing and deserved reputation of a number of national and international airline carriers for significantly improving the level of their customer service, a business strategy which includes a 10 per cent over-booking policy contains all the ingredients for disaffected passengers. Or the major hotel chains who, despite demanding confirmed room reservations, then subject the guest to producing two means of identification and an imprint of his credit card. Notwithstanding the resources committed to training front of house staff and glitzing up the reception area, most hotels continue to be, in the immortal words of Alan Bennett, 'theatres of embarrassment'.

Customer service programmes that simply concentrate on staff at the customer interface, without regard to the business infrastructure, have rightly been stigmatised as providers of 'smile training'.

A passionate advocate of service and quality training starting within the core of the organization is Mike Scally, joint managing director of Lifeskills. He says that 'the quality of service that reaches the customer begins with the quality of service that staff give to each other'.

REWARDING AND RECOGNIZING THE SERVICE HEROES AND HEROINES

Thirdly, reward and recognize excellence. One of the most powerful ways of reinforcing a positive attitude among staff to quality and service is to reward and recognize high performance. An essential element in that process is the setting and measuring of standards of service.

While the number of companies introducing Total Quality Management or Customer Care programmes has reached an all time high the number who have attempted to make the link between quality and service targets and reward has been surprisingly low. However, among those that have, a number display a commendable degree of innovation and understanding of the power of reward.

A recent Incomes Data Study[2] featured a number of such companies including Rank Xerox, Elida Gibbs and British Steel.

Rank Xerox

One of the earlier entrants into the quality and service arena, in the mid 1980s the Xerox corporation launched a quality programme called Leadership Through Quality, in which there was a clear shift of emphasis from improving internal quality to improving the quality of service given to customers.

A key feature of the approach adopted by Rank Xerox has been the use of independent market research, the three key surveys being as follows:

- *90 Day Survey* – This involves a random survey of new installations, 90 days after the equipment was installed. It comprises of a simple checklist of initial service and aftercare, and aimed to measure customer dissatisfaction. The target is clearly nought per cent dissatisfaction.

- *Customer Satisfaction Management Survey* – The CSMS surveys a cross-section of existing and new customers between once and three times a year. The customers are asked around 40 specific questions about the products themselves, as well as the service received, which allows information to be fed back to manufacturing and research and development for improvements to product design and manufacture.

- *Competitive Survey* – This annual survey attempts to measure Rank Xerox's performance against it's competitors. A sample of Xerox and non-Xerox customers are asked a number of simple questions about their office equipment, from which Rank Xerox are able to determine where it stands in relation to other companies. The objective is to be number one in each of the eight business areas in each country. The eight business areas are high, mid and low volume reprographic; high, mid and low volume electronic printing; fax machines and electronic typewriters.

All three surveys were cascaded down to all operating companies in the group.

Since 1986 each of the three surveys have influenced the organization's approach to reward and have, in different forms, triggered payment. For Senior Management a 5 per cent customer service bonus is available, payment being generated by performance against the 90 Day Survey results. In 1989 the bonus was extended to around 2000 middle managers throughout the Rank Xerox group. For this group, a customer satisfaction element worth 2.5 per cent of salary was introduced. The scheme was run along the same lines as the 1989 senior manager scheme, with the customer satisfaction bonus paid quarterly and a proportion paid at the end of the year, depending on the Competitive Survey Results.

A similar scheme based on the Competitive Survey has now been introduced for all Rank Xerox group headquarters staff.

Commenting on the scheme the company points out that since its introduction there have been improvements in the overall level of customer satisfaction and a corresponding improvement in profit and revenue. In terms of hard data the customer satisfaction figures have increased from 92 per cent in the first quarter of 1990, to 95 per cent in the second quarter of 1991.

Elida Gibbs

Elida Gibbs the Yorkshire-based Unilever subsidiary produces and distributes a wide range of toiletries and personal hygiene products.

Since their major customers have the right to reject any delivery which does not contain the correct mix of products, balanced production and right-first-time customer service are critical.

Two bonus schemes operate within the company, one relating to the level of customer service achieved, the other based on reducing the cost of waste.

The customer service measurement is simply the percentage of orders sent out right first time, with the bonus payment being made when the target service level is met or exceeded. The scheme pays out a maximum of ten days' pay when maximum performance is achieved. As the service levels have improved so have the targets that generate payment. In 1989 a payment of three days' pay was generated by achieving a performance level of 93 per cent, rising to ten days' pay at 98 per cent. In 1991 the targets had increased to two days' pay at 96 per cent, rising to ten days' pay for achieving a customer service rating of 99 per cent.

The second scheme is based on the reduction in the cost of waste and for each half of 1991 a bonus of one day's pay was set for each £100,000 reduction in the cost of waste to a maximum of £500,000. The results of both schemes have been impressive and from a low of 88 per cent in the third quarter of 1988 the customer service level has increased to between 98 per cent and 99 per cent throughout the whole of 1990 and 1991.

British Steel

In British Steel Strip Products local bonus schemes have been in operation since the early 1980s. The bonus that emanates from the scheme is paid quarterly, in arrears, and applies to all employees from the works managers to the shop floor. The scheme reflects performance in four key areas as follows:

1. *Productivity* – this is a direct measure of the man-hours required per tonne of steel produced in the relevant quarter.
2. *Product cost* – as the product cost falls, the bonus increases on a sliding scale. Product cost is the cost of cold rolled coil.
3. *Delivery-to-time* – the bonus increases on a sliding scale as the percentage of deliveries made on time increases. For example, at one works, for every 2 per cent increase in deliveries-to-time above 80 per cent, a one 1 cent bonus is paid.
4. *Quality* – at one works, this is a measure of the amount of prime (top quality) product produced, as a percentage of the liquid steel used in the production process. The higher the percentage

of prime product, the less non-prime product has been made and the less liquid steel had been wasted in the various stages of production. As the prime percentage increases, so does the bonus. At another works however, the measure is of the amount of steel wasted, rejected or downgraded. As the tonnage of wastage falls, the bonus rises.

When the schemes were established payment levels were around 4.5 per cent; they are currently averaging around 10 per cent, although they have been as high as 15–18 per cent. But there is a wide variation, from plant to plant and from quarter to quarter in the level of bonus payments made under the schemes, due to a number of internal and external factors.

British Steel believes that the bonus schemes have been highly successful not just in improving productivity but in encouraging a new culture in the business. In particular the company would argue that employees are more interested in their work's performance to the extent that they always have a pretty accurate idea of how they are faring and what their bonus is likely to be.

In addition, IDS would emphasize the fact that after more than ten years the schemes, albeit with modifications, continue to assist in achieving performance improvements and this is further testament to their success. Usually, schemes have a finite life, after which the payments are fully consolidated and the schemes are dropped.

Joshua Tetley

Within Joshua Tetley several different schemes have been introduced to encourage and recognize excellence in customer service whether internal or external. These include:

- *Customer Service Quality Award* – Each quarter the steering committee invites service team leaders to nominate an individual in the company who has shown exceptional service to others. The winner is presented with an inscribed cut-glass trophy and invited to take his partner for an evening meal at the company's expense.

- *Distribution Reward and Recognition System* – Some two years ago the company introduced a reward and recognition package for employees in the distribution fleet. The scheme is based on the customer service level achieved, measured by reference to:

'Did the customer receive the requested brands in the ordered quantity on the specified day'. At the start of the programme the average service level was 90 per cent. A level that is judged to be good in comparison with our competitors in the industry. However, we need to turn conventional wisdom on its head: in a quality company those statistics are interpreted as meaning that 10 per cent of customers either didn't receive their delivery on the specified day or didn't receive the specified quantity, or the requested brand. A totally different perspective, and not one for self congratulation.

A point that has escaped The Royal Mail in that they recently announced in a self congratulating manner that they have increased the percentage of first class letters delivered by the next working day from 75 per cent in 1989 to 86 per cent in 1991. While one wouldn't wish to decry the efforts that have obviously gone into achieving that improvement, they would have appeared to have missed the point that since they deliver 15 billion letters a year, 21 million letters are delivered late, each failing to meet the contract we, as individual consumers, enter into when we pay the higher postal rate for next day delivery.

Since the reward and recognition scheme commenced in distribution, customer service levels have increased to an average of between 95 and 96 per cent and our target is to emulate our East Yorkshire depot which in January 1991 achieved a service level of 99.4 per cent.

- *Bar Staff and Manager of the Month Award* – Award winners are selected by trade directors and area managers from nominations received from either within the trade or from customers. The criteria for selecting the winners is simply based on which individual was the best example of quality service in action.

MEASURING SERVICE

The fourth ingredient enabling companies to implement effective quality and service initiatives is, 'what gets measured gets done'. To be effective you need to establish credible measurements of both service and quality prior to introducing any customer service initiative, and you need to regularly review the progress that you are making.

One of the most fundamental and yet least understood philosophies of management is that measurement improves performance. As an example, a key statistic for breweries is the amount of beers and lagers returned to the brewery by its customer. At the start of the Quality Pays programme, beer returns were running at around 1 per cent and, since we brew and distribute over one million barrels, it will be appreciated how significant the cost of returned beer is. Today our returns are 0.3 per cent and our target is 0.1 per cent.

The 100 Club

Equally, in a service organization the way we greet customers is important. One of the most important elements in customer trans-actions is the use of the customer's name, and in that respect as part of this programme the company introduced the 100 Club. To get membership of the 100 Club, members of staff in our pubs have to be able to recall the name of a customer and something credible about him or her.

We believed when we started the programme that if individuals could relate to 100 customers, they would have done extremely well. Today we have 500 members of the 100 Club, 300 members of the 250 Club, 200 members of the 500 club and 50 members of the 1000 club. The individual ability to excel in the recall of names, as on the Olympic track, knows no limits. Carol Grisdale, Manageress of the Fox & Grapes pub achieved the UK record when she was able to relate to and identify 2000 customers. In addition to having a phenomenal memory, Carol says her achievement was stimulated by 'having targets to beat and the recognition received from the company as well as from customers – knowing customers names means bigger tips'.

As a customer isn't it more satisfying when service staff use your name naturally and spontaneously? It's certainly a preferable alternative to the 'musak greeting' we so often encounter: 'good evening sir, my name is Mandy, I'm your waitress, have a good meal'. Staff exhibit resistance to this form of stereotype greeting which for the customer contains all the sincerity of the 'have a nice day' syndrome. The Government's recently announced Citizens Charter initiative contained the provision that public servants should no longer be anonymous. In future those who come into contact with the public will be expected to wear name badges and to give their names on the telephone or in writing. Whilst this initiative is to be welcomed, an even more positive illustration of commitment to customer service in the public sector would be the training of staff to use the names of those members of the public they regularly come into contact with. Those with a natural talent already do so as I know from my experience of occasionally travelling on the morning York to Kings Cross Pullman. The regular chief steward on that train has picked up my name from my Visa card and when I enter the dining car greets me by name. Or Franco, the former head waiter at the Roman Court restaurant in Burn Bridge, Harrogate, who not only has an amazing ability to recall customers names but equally was able, after a couple of visits, to remember their favourite tipple. I well recall taking a friend from America into the restaurant and Franco automatically asked my wife and I if we would like our normal drink which, un-prompted, he then proceeded to pour. He then asked my visitor what he would like to drink. He replied 'I'll have my usual', Franco paused and said 'I know, it's malt whisky, it's Glenfiddich, but I can't recall whether it's ice or water?' Now, this was only my guest's second visit to the restaurant, the first occasion being four months earlier! Staff like that are a real asset to any business, because we recall the service long after the quality of the meal has been forgotten.

Measuring customer satisfaction

At the risk of stating the obvious it is important to measure customer reaction and satisfaction levels on the service and quality we provide. Within Joshua Tetley one of the mechanisms used is the customer care card illustrated on page 204.

Since the customer care card was introduced some two years ago over 20,000 have been completed and returned to us. The cards are freely available in our pubs and restaurants and over 96 per cent are returned with genuine comments and details of occupation, address etc. The comments on service and product quality enable us to track with the licensees the standards being offered. As will be seen from Figure 13.2, the customer ratings are very good. It is a great source of satisfaction that customers want to tell you when you get it right as well as when you do not.

One very useful by-product of the scheme is the amount of data we are able to capture on the customer profile for each of our pubs. It equally provides an excellent mechanism for rewarding individuals who consistently achieve high customer satisfaction ratings.

CUSTOMER CARE SURVEY

Our aim is to provide you with the best quality products and service. We would like you to tell us how we've done today.

Paul Tatton
Retail Sales Director

Pub .... No. ....

Day of Visit ....

Time of Visit ....

Age: 18-24   25-35   36-45   45+

Name: Mr/Mrs/Miss .... Occupation ....

Address ....

Town .... Postcode ....

	Excellent	Good	Average	Poor
Exterior				
Welcome				
Decor				
Menu				
Service				
Drinks				
Food				
Staff				

Can you suggest any way in which we could improve bar or service facilities?

Will you come back again?   Yes/No

Thank you for taking the trouble to answer our questions. Please return – postage is free.

Figure 13.1   Measuring customer satisfaction

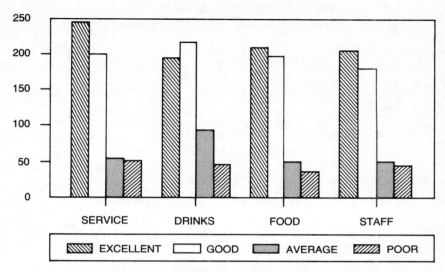

Figure 13.2   Care card analysis – summary June 1991

Surveying the personnel contribution

It is also important that in-house service providers continually check with their internal customers the level of service they are providing. Since July 1989 the retail personnel department has, on a quarterly basis, been surveying the opinions of area managers on the quality of service they provide on selection, training, administration and customer care. The questions asked in the survey form are as follows:

SELECTION

When assisting with interviews in the department:
1. Did you receive the candidate's application form in adequate time?
2. Was the interviewing environment comfortable – if not, why not?
3. Did you receive feedback on the interview results from the selection team?
4. Were you kept informed of the candidates progress throughout the remainder of the interview process?
5. For couples you have recruited was the selection profile feedback:

Poor		Adequate		Excellent
1	2	3	4	5

6. Will you use this information to manage your new recruits?
7. Is the information contained on the talent bank file:

Insufficient		Acceptable		Comprehensive
1	2	3	4	5

8. Is the help received from the selection team during the recruitment process:

Insufficient		Acceptable		Great
1	2	3	4	5

TRAINING

1. Has the in-house training with the trainer manager:

Hindered				Helped
1	2	3	4	5

2. Do you perceive the training report as being of:

Little Value			Great Value	
1	2	3	4	5

3. Did the training team communicate with you regularly during the organization of the trainees' induction programme?
4. If appropriate, when you visited your couple at Ashfield House Training Centre did you consider it:

A waste of time			Very beneficial	
1	2	3	4	5

5. Is you training officer generally accessible in order to discuss general training issues?

Never		Occasionally		Always
1	2	3	4	5

6. How important do you believe *Immediate* in-house/off-site training is for all new starters?

Important			Extremely important	
1	2	3	4	5

ADMINISTRATION

1. How helpful are we?

Unhelpful			Helpful	
1	2	3	4	5

2. If you requested an offer letter, how soon was it returned to you for signature?

	Same Day	Within 24 Hours	Over 2 Days

3. How pleasant is our telephone manner?

Unpleasant		Acceptable		Very Pleasant
1	2	3	4	5

4. How soon after leaving a message is your call returned?

It isn't		Next Day		Same Day
1	2	3	4	5

5. When you visit the department does everybody have time for you?

No		Sometimes		Always
1	2	3	4	5

Based on the one to five rating scale the overall results achieved in July 1989 averaged 3.2, and in July 1991 had increased to 4.1.

The fundamental point to make on all the examples using measurement is that *measurement stimulates the achievement. None of us is an achiever until someone expects something of us.*

PUBLICIZING THE PROGRAMME

A further important aspect of maintaining the momentum of quality and service initiatives is to publicize the progress that is being made. In addition to including articles on quality and service in our general employee publications, Joshua Tetley produce a half-yearly magazine devoted solely to Quality Pays.

It is important to point out that all our publicity has been in-house and we have not directly communicated our Quality Pays programme to our external customers. Broadcasting your programme to customers is something to be avoided. If you want a classic example of this misguided approach then you only have to look at the 'Getting There' campaign by British Rail in the late 1980s. This involved BR in heavyweight TV advertising focusing on customer service. The reality was that they raised customers' expectations before they were able to deliver, the net result being more, not less, dissatisfied passengers.

SELECTING QUALITY PEOPLE

The sixth ingredient: increasingly, companies that embark on quality and service programmes will have to accept that the quality of the people they employ sets the limits on the level of service they can offer customers. *Good service is giving people a little more than they expect, and excellent service is enjoying giving people a little more than they expect.* The crucial test is the ability to select individuals who find fulfillment and enjoyment from being of service to others.

The six key ingredients we have discussed should enable companies to avoid some of the pitfalls of the quality and service initiatives that commenced in the early 1980s and sadly, many of which failed. More importantly following these six key ingredients should enable companies to develop a culture which, in the long term, will enthusiastically embrace the philosophy and practice of serving the customer right.

SUMMARY

In this chapter we concluded that:

- Quality and service programmes need to be owned by top management, who need to create and seize opportunities to demonstrate their commitment.

- Reward and recognition systems which focus on the attainment of quality and service standards are a powerful means of maintaining employee commitment to the programme.

- Regularly measuring the level of service and quality achieved within the organization and experienced by the customer enables companies to systematically track progress, identify potential problems and confound the cynics.

- The limits to the level of service and quality we can aspire to and achieve in practice will be determined by the quality of the people we employ.

THE SIX ISSUES FOR THE BOARD AGENDA

1. Quality and service are at the top of our board agenda displacing departmental profit and loss accounts from the number one spot since we fully understand that it is quality and service that generate profit, not the reverse.

2. The marketing function needs to regularly and consistently provide data which enables us to evaluate the level of service and product quality experienced by the customer compared with the level we are aspiring to.

3. We fully understand the cost of poor service and the lifetime value of the customer.

4. We are as equally committed to retaining established customers as gaining new ones.

5. We positively recruit into the organization those individuals who find satisfaction and fulfillment from being of service to others.

6. We are able to identify our quality and service heroes and heroines and positively reward and recognize their achievement.

As we come to the conclusion of this book it is timely to remind ourselves of the essential strands that support our talent equation, the essential elements which will enable us to put success back on the boardroom agenda.

- Study success.

- Select talent.

- Reward and recognize high performance.

- Create a winning team.

- Commit the organization to becoming a quality company.

Five key components that will ensure that our business continues to grow and prosper beyond the year 2000, and we have something meaningful to bequeath to the next generation of managers. The route may at times be difficult, it may at times be slower than the quick fixes advocated by false prophets, but the prescription can make a difference to our organization, a substantial difference for the better.

As we all grapple with our day to day problems and attempt to become a talent led organization, we need continually to remind ourselves that putting success back on the boardroom agenda is a journey, not a destination.

REFERENCES

1 Coulson-Thomas, C (1992) 'Surveying the Scene', *Total Quality Management*, IFS Publications, Bedford, February.
2 IDS Study 492 (October 1991), 'Bonus Schemes Part 2', Income Data Services Ltd.

This book has been based on research I undertook for the following articles, for which acknowledgement is made.

'A Scientific Approach To Selection'	*Personnel Management*, Oct 1987
'How To Pick The Winners'	*Sunday Times*, 1 May 1988
'Age Of The Innovators In Personnel'	*Sunday Times*, 23 Oct 1988
'The Rules For Success In The 1990's'	*Sunday Times*, 7 May 1989
'In Pursuit Of Talent'	*International Journal Of Hospitality Management*, Vol 8 No 2, 2 June 1989
'Age Of The New Image Employer'	*Sunday Times*, 2 July 1989
'How To Swing Unused Talent Into Action'	*Sunday Times*, 20 Aug 1989
'Why The Best Man Doesn't Always Win'	*Sunday Times*, 3 Dec 1989
'Ten Steps To Success'	*Executive Development*, Vol 3 No 1, 1990
'How Clever Negotiators Get Their Way'	*Sunday Times*, 21 Jan 1990
'Why Talent Ranks Before Training'	*Sunday Times*, 18 Mar 1990
'Job Hopping Up The Ladder'	*Sunday Times*, 3 June 1990
'Serving The Customer Right'	*Sunday Times*, 1 July 1990
'Restive Executives Find Escape Route'	*Sunday Times*, 13 Jan 1991
'Take Care With Corporate Slimming'	*Sunday Times*, 17 Feb 1991
'Cheers (Quality Pays In Joshua Tetley)'	*Managing Service Quality*, IFS Publications, May 1991
'Managing To Survive In A Changing World'	*Sunday Times*, 9 June 1991
'Growing Faith In The Workforce'	*Yorkshire Post*, Business Weekly, 21 July 1992
'From Engineer To Grocer's Daughter'	*Managing Service Quality*, IFS Publications, Sept 1992

Index

and fostering of competition
122–3, 128
of high performance 61
for hourly paid staff 125–6
and motivation of talent 114, 118,
128
negative 127–8
personal thank you messages 118,
119, 128
prizes 124
and publicity 122, 126
social events 123–4, 128
see also reward
recruitment
constant 44–5
and establishment of 'talent
bank' 44–5, 56, 58
of most talented employees 58
new procedures needed 12,
27–30, 34
and 'poaching' 43–4
predictions versus actual
performance 58
and 'selling the company' 138–9
Taco-Bell Company 52
traditional systems 12
see also interviews
redundancy programmes, and loss
of talent 46
Reed International 73
referrals of talent 43–4
relator, as life theme 37
Rentokill 181
Research Surveys of Great Britain
181
responsibility, as life theme 37
restrictive practices 65, 104, 107
retail partnership, at Joshua Tetley
100–2
retirement
early 143
into the job 150
management attitudes to 143
reward
appropriate 124–5

aspirational nature of 76, 80–1,
84
for board and executive
management 109–12
cascading down through
organisations 91–9
changes in attitude to 77, 79–83,
106
five principles of 84
and hidden talent 79–80
for high performance 12, 14–15,
61, 197–201
for hourly paid staff 125–6,
197–201
influence of 113
influences on 61–76
necessary changes to systems 20
performance-driven 87–9
for repetitive work 62
role in empowerment 97–102,
113
service-related 86–7
structured payment system 14
see also recognition
Ritz Carlton Hotels, use of
structured interviews 52
Robinson, Derek 68
Roddick, Anita 181
Roman Court restaurant,
Harrogate 203
Rothermere, Viscount 73
Rowland, 'Tiny' 73
Royal Commission on Trade
Unions and Employers
Associations 65–6
Royal Mail, customer service levels
201
Rush, Myron, biblical approach to
management 165

safety standards 104, 105
Sainsbury, David 73
Sainsbury, J, plc 73
Sainsbury, Lord, of Preston
Candover 73

Tesco supermarket group, 'Mystery
Shopper' programme 78
Tetley, Joshua
100 Club 202–3
adoption of new payment and
reward systems 85–113
advertising 39–43, 56
awarded 'National Brewery
Chain of the Year' (1992) 102
Bar Staff and Manager of the
Month Award 201
bonus schemes 87–9, 90–1, 92–3,
94
cascading reward down 91–9
communication and consultation
184
costs of staff turnover 168–9
customer care card 203–5
customer perceptions of 193–5
customer service orientation 35,
36, 56, 184
Customer Service Quality Award
200
data on talent factor 13
development of talent 167–8
Diploma in Business
Administration (DBA) 163–4
Distribution Reward and
Recognition System 200–1
graduate employment 48
management structure 86–7
overtime reduction scheme 106–8
payment systems 184
performance reviews 87–9
'Quality Pays' programme
184–94, 202
recognition and motivation 118,
120–4
recruitment of women 48
relationship with trade unions
184
Retail Partnership Scheme
100–2, 113
reward structure for board and
executive management 109–12

selection systems 184
staff turnover 47, 167
structured interviews 38, 39,
45–6, 47–8, 56
survey of attitudes to promotion
144–5
survey of top 25 managers 46–7,
155
training and development 163–4,
167–8, 184
thank you messages 118, 119–21
Thanos Group (hotel operators) 44
Thatcher, Margaret 67, 69
Thatcherism
and human resource
management 11
and industrial relations 67–9
Thomas, George, Viscount
Tonypandy 115–16
Thompson, Clive 181
Thompson, Sir Peter 73
time and motion study 62
Total Quality Management (TQM)
197
trade unions
at Joshua Tetley 184
in brewing industry 91–2
and closed shops 67
and collective bargaining 75
distribution 103, 104
influence on pay policies 65
power of shop stewards 62
Royal Commission on 65–6
and Thatcherism 67–9
training 12, 14, 15
analysis of effectiveness 155–6,
157, 173, 206
in association with polytechnics
and colleges 162–4
at Joshua Tetley 188
dissatisfaction with 19, 158, 162
government initiatives 152–3, 156
incentive schemes for 112
induction 167–8
investment in 152–3, 156–7, 173